# ROUGHING IT IN THE BUSH;

OR,

# LIFE IN CANADA.

BY SUSANNA MOODIE.

I sketch from Nature, and the picture's true;
Whate'er the subject, whether grave or gay,
Painful experience in a distant land
Made it mine own.

*IN TWO PARTS....PART II.*

NINTH THOUSAND.

New York:
GEORGE P. PUTNAM, 10 PARK PLACE.
M.DCCC.LIV.

# CONTENTS OF VOL. II.

# ROUGHING IT IN THE BUSH.

## CHAPTER I.

### A JOURNEY TO THE WOODS.

**'Tis well for us poor denizens of earth**
**That God conceals the future from our gaze;**
**Or Hope, the blessed watcher on Life's tower,**
**Would fold her wings, and on the dreary waste**
**Close the bright eye that through the murky clouds**
**Of blank Despair still sees the glorious sun.**

IT was a bright, frosty morning when I bade adieu to the farm, the birthplace of my little Agnes, who, nestled beneath my cloak, was sweetly sleeping on my knee, unconscious of the long journey before us into the wilderness. The sun had not as yet risen. Anxious to get to our place of destination before dark, we started as early as we could. Our own fine team had been sold the day before for forty pounds; and one of our neighbours, a Mr. D——, was to convey us and our household goods to Douro for the sum of twenty dollars. During the week he had made several journeys, with furniture and stores; and all that now remained was to be conveyed to the woods in two large lumber-sleighs, one driven by himself, the other by a younger brother.

It was not without regret that I left Melsetter, for so my husband had called the place, after his father's estate in Orkney. It was a beautiful, picturesque spot; and, in spite of the evil neighbourhood, I had learned to love it; indeed, it was much against my wish that it was sold. I had a great dislike to removing, which involves a necessary loss, and is apt to give to the emigrant roving and unsettled habits. But all regrets were now useless; and happily unconscious of the life of toil and anxiety that awaited us in those dreadful woods, I tried my best to be cheerful, and to regard the future with a hopeful eye.

Our driver was a shrewd, clever man, for his opportunities. He took charge of the living cargo, which consisted of my husband, our maid-servant, the two little children, and myself—besides a large hamper, full of poultry—a dog, and a cat. The lordly sultan of the imprisoned seraglio thought fit to conduct himself in a very eccentric manner, for at every barnyard we happened to pass, he clapped his wings, and crowed so long and loud that it afforded great amusement to the whole party, and doubtless was very edifying to the poor hens, who lay huddled together as mute as mice.

"That 'ere rooster thinks he's on the top of the heap," said our driver, laughing. "I guess he's not used to travelling in a close conveyance. Listen! How all the crowers in the neighbourhood give him back a note of defiance! But he knows that he's safe enough at the bottom of the basket."

The day was so bright for the time of year (the first week in February), that we suffered no inconvenience from the cold. Little Katie was enchanted with the jingling of the sleigh-bells, and, nestled among the packages, kept singing or talking to the horses in her baby lingo. Trifling as these little incidents were, before we had proceeded ten miles on our long journey, they revived my drooping spirits, and I began to feel a lively interest in the scenes through which we were passing.

The first twenty miles of the way was over a hilly and well-cleared country; and as in winter the deep snow fills up the inequalities, and makes all roads alike, we glided as swiftly and steadily along as if they had been the best highways in the world. Anon, the clearings began to diminish, and tall woods arose on either side of the path; their solemn aspect, and the deep silence that brooded over their vast solitudes, inspiring the mind with a strange awe. Not a breath of wind stirred the leafless branches, whose huge shadows, reflected upon the dazzling white covering of snow, lay so perfectly still, that it seemed as if Nature had suspended her operations, that life and motion had ceased, and that she was sleeping in her winding-sheet, upon the bier of death.

"I guess you will find the woods pretty lonesome," said our driver, whose thoughts had been evidently employed on the same subject as our own. "We were once in the woods, but emigration has stepped ahead of us, and made our'n a cleared part of the country. When I was a boy, all this country, for thirty miles on every side of us, was bush land. As to Peterborough, the place was unknown; not a settler had ever passed through the great swamp, and some of them believed that it was the end of the world."

"What swamp is that?" asked I.

"Oh, the great Cavan swamp. We are just two miles from it; and I tell you the horses will need a good rest, and ourselves a good dinner, by the time we are through it. Ah! Mrs. Moodie, if ever you travel that way in summer, you will know something about corduroy roads. I was 'most jolted to death last fall; I thought it would have been no bad notion to have insured my teeth before I left C——. I really expected that they would have been shook out of my head before we had done manœuvring over the big logs."

"How will my crockery stand it in the next sleigh?" quoth I. "If the road is such as you describe, I am afraid that I shall not bring a whole plate to Douro."

"Oh! the snow is a great leveller—it makes all rough places smooth. But with regard to this swamp, I have something to tell you. About ten years ago, no one had ever seen the other side of it; and if pigs or cattle strayed away into it, they fell a prey to the wolves and bears, and were seldom recovered.

"An old Scotch emigrant, who had located himself on this side of it, so often lost his beasts that he determined during the summer season to try and explore the place, and see if there were any end to it. So he takes an axe on his shoulder, and a bag of provisions for the week, not forgetting a flask of whiskey, and off he starts all alone, and tells his wife that if he never returned, she and little Jock must try and carry on the farm without him; but he was determined to see the end of the swamp, even if it led to the other world. He fell upon a fresh cattle-track, which he followed all that day; and towards night he found himself in the heart of a tangled wilderness of bushes, and himself half eaten up with mosquitoes and black-flies. He was more than tempted to give in, and return home by the first glimpse of light.

"The Scotch are a tough people; they are not easily daunted—a few difficulties only seem to make them more eager to get on; and he felt ashamed the next moment, as he told me, of giving up. So he finds out a large, thick cedar-tree for his bed, climbs up, and coiling himself among the branches like a bear, he was soon fast asleep.

"The next morning, by daylight, he continued his journey, not forgetting to blaze with his axe the trees to the right and left as he went along. The ground was so spongy and wet that at every step he plunged up to his knees in water, but he seemed no nearer the end of the swamp than he had been the day before. He saw several deer, a raccoon, and a ground-hog, during his walk, but was unmolested by bears or wolves. Having passed through several creeks, and killed a great many snakes, he felt so weary towards the second day that he determined to go home the next morning. But just as he began to think his search was fruitless, he observed that the cedars and tamaracks which had obstructed his path became less numerous, and were succeeded by bass and soft maple. The ground, also, became less moist, and he was soon ascending a rising slope, covered with oak and beech, which shaded land of the very best quality. The old man was now fully convinced that he had cleared the great swamp; and that, instead of leading to the other world, it had conducted him to a country that would yield the very best returns for cultivation. His favourable report led to the formation of the road that we are about to cross, and to the settlement of Peterborough, which is one of the most promising new settlements in this district, and is surrounded by a splendid back country."

We were descending a very steep hill, and encountered an ox-sleigh, which was crawling slowly up it in a contrary direction. Three people were seated at the bottom of the vehicle upon straw, which made a cheap substitute for buffalo robes. Perched, as we were, upon the crown of the height, we looked completely down into the sleigh, and during the whole course of my life I never saw three uglier mortals collected into such a narrow space. The man was blear-eyed, with a hare-lip, through which protruded two dreadful yellow teeth which resembled the tusks of a boar. The woman was long-faced, high cheek-boned, red-haired, and freckled all over like a toad. The boy resembled his hideous mother, but with the addition of a villainous obliquity of vision which rendered him the most disgusting object in this singular trio.

As we passed them, our driver gave a knowing nod to my husband, directing, at the same time, the most quizzical glance towards the strangers, as he exclaimed, "We are in luck, sir! I think that 'ere sleigh may be called Beauty's egg-basket!"

We made ourselves very merry at the poor people's expense, and Mr. D——, with his odd stories and Yankeefied expressions, amused the tedium of our progress through the great swamp, which in summer presents for several miles one uniform bridge of rough and unequal logs, all laid loosely across huge sleepers, so that they jumped up and down, when pressed by the wheels, like the keys of a piano. The rough motion and jolting occasioned by this collision is so distressing that it never fails to entail upon the traveller sore bones and an aching head for the rest of the day. The path is so narrow over these logs that two wagons cannot pass without great difficulty, which is rendered more dangerous by the deep natural ditches on either side of the bridge, formed by broad creeks that flow out of the swamp, and often terminate in mud-holes of very ominous dimensions. The snow, however, hid from us all the ugly features of the road, and Mr. D—— steered us through it in perfect safety, and landed us at the door of a little log house which crowned the steep hill on the other side of the swamp, and which he dignified with the name of a tavern.

It was now two o'clock. We had been on the road since seven; and men, women, and children were all ready for the good dinner that Mr. D—— had promised us at this splendid house of entertainment, where we were destined to stay for two hours, to refresh ourselves and rest the horses.

"Well, Mrs. J——, what have you got for our dinner?"

said the driver, after he had seen to the accommodation of his teams.

"Pritters and pork, sir. Nothing else to be had in the woods. Thank God, we have enough of that!"

D—— shrugged up his shoulders, and looked at us.

"We've plenty of that same at home. But hunger's good sauce. Come, be spry, widow, and see about it, for I am very hungry."

I inquired for a private room for myself and the children, but there were no private rooms in the house. The apartment we occupied was like the cobbler's stall in the old song, and I was obliged to attend upon them in public.

"You have much to learn, ma'am, if you are going to the woods," said Mrs. J——.

"To unlearn, you mean," said Mr. D——. "To tell you the truth, Mrs. Moodie, ladies and gentlemen have no business in the woods. Eddication spoils man or woman for that location. So, widow (turning to our hostess), you are not tired of living alone yet?"

"No, sir; I have no wish for a second husband. I had enough of the first. I like to have my own way—to lie down mistress, and get up master."

"You don't like to be put out of your *old* way," returned he, with a mischievous glance.

She coloured very red; but it might be the heat of the fire over which she was frying the pork for our dinner.

I was very hungry, but I felt no appetite for the dish she was preparing for us. It proved salt, hard, and unsavoury.

D—— pronounced it very bad, and the whiskey still worse, with which he washed it down.

I asked for a cup of tea and a slice of bread. But they were out of tea, and the hop-rising had failed, and there was no bread in the house. For this disgusting meal we paid at the rate of a quarter of a dollar a-head.

I was glad when, the horses being again put to, we escaped from the rank odour of the fried pork, and were once more in the fresh air.

"Well, mister; did not you grudge your money for that bad meat?" said D——, when we were once more seated in the sleigh. "But in these parts, the worse the fare the higher the charge."

"I would not have cared," said I, "if I could have got a cup of tea."

"Tea! it's poor trash. I never could drink tea in my life. But I like coffee, when 'tis boiled till it's quite black. But coffee is not good without plenty of trimmings."

"What do you mean by trimmings?"

He laughed. "Good sugar, and sweet cream. Coffee is not worth drinking without trimmings."

Often in after years have I recalled the coffee trimmings, when endeavouring to drink the vile stuff which goes by the name of coffee in the houses of entertainment in the country.

We had now passed through the narrow strip of clearing which surrounded the tavern, and again entered upon the woods. It was near sunset, and we were rapidly descending a steep hill, when one of the traces that held our sleigh suddenly broke. D—— pulled up in order to repair the damage. His brother's team was close behind, and our unexpected stand-still brought the horses upon us before J. D—— could stop them. I received so violent a blow from the head of one of them, just in the back of the neck, that for a few minutes I was stunned and insensible. When I recovered, I was supported in the arms of my husband, over whose knees I was leaning, and D—— was rubbing my hands and temples with snow.

"There, Mr. Moodie, she's coming to. I thought she was killed. I have seen a man before now killed by a blow from a horse's head in the like manner." As soon as we could, we resumed our places in the sleigh; but all enjoyment of our journey, had it been otherwise possible, was gone.

When we reached Peterborough, Moodie wished us to remain at the inn all night, as we had still eleven miles of our journey to perform, and that through a blazed forest-road, little travelled, and very much impeded by fallen trees and other obstacles; but D—— was anxious to get back as soon as possible to his own home, and he urged us very pathetically to proceed.

The moon arose during our stay at the inn, and gleamed upon the straggling frame houses which then formed the now populous and thriving town of Peterborough. We crossed the wild, rushing, beautiful Otonabee river by a rude bridge, and soon found ourselves journeying over the plains or level heights beyond the village, which were thinly wooded with picturesque groups of oak and pine, and very much resembled a gentleman's park at home. Far below, to our right (for we were upon the Smith-town side) we heard the rushing of the river, whose rapid waters never receive curb from the iron chain of winter. Even while the rocky banks are coated with ice, and the frost-king suspends from every twig and branch the most beautiful and fantastic crystals, the black waters rush foaming along, a thick steam rising constantly above the rapids, as from a boiling pot. The shores vibrate and tremble beneath the force of the impetuous flood, as it whirls round cedar-crowned islands and opposing rocks, and hurries on to pour its tribute into the Rice Lake, to swell the calm, majestic grandeur of the Trent, till its waters are lost in the beautiful bay of Quinté, and finally merged in the blue ocean of Ontario.

The most renowned of our English rivers dwindle into little muddy rills when compared with the sublimity of the Canadian waters. No language can adequately express the solemn grandeur of her lake and river scenery; the glorious islands that float, like visions from fairy land, upon the bosom of these azure mirrors of her cloudless skies. No dreary breadth of marshes, covered with flags, hide from our gaze the expanse of heaven-tinted waters; no foul mud-banks spread their unwholesome exhalations around. The rocky shores are crowned with the cedar, the birch, the alder, and soft maple, that dip their long tresses in the pure stream; from every crevice in the limestone the harebell and Canadian rose wave their graceful blossoms.

The fiercest droughts of summer may diminish the volume and power of these romantic streams, but it never leaves their rocky channels bare, nor checks the mournful music of their dancing waves. Through the openings in the forest, we now and then caught the silver gleam of the river tumbling on in moonlight splendour, while the hoarse chiding of the wind in the lofty pines above us gave a fitting response to the melancholy cadence of the waters.

The children had fallen asleep. A deep silence pervaded the party. Night was above us with her mysterious stars. The ancient forest stretched around us on every side, and a foreboding sadness sunk upon my heart. Memory was busy with the events of many years. I retraced step by step the pilgrimage of my past life, until arriving at that passage in its sombre history, I gazed through tears upon the singularly savage scene around me, and secretly marvelled, "What brought me here?"

"Providence," was the answer which the soul gave. "Not for your own welfare, perhaps, but for the welfare of your children, the unerring hand of the great Father has led you here. You form a connecting link in the destinies of many. It is impossible for any human creature to live for himself alone. It may be your lot to suffer, but others will reap a benefit from your trials. Look up with confidence to Heaven, and the sun of hope will yet shed a cheering beam through the forbidden depths of this tangled wilderness."

The road became so bad that Mr. D—— was obliged to dismount, and lead his horses through the more intricate passages. The animals themselves, weary with their long journey and heavy load, proceeded at foot-fall. The moon, too, had deserted us, and the only light we had to guide us through the dim arches of the forest was from the snow and the stars, which now peered down upon us through the leafless branches of the trees, with uncommon brilliancy.

"It will be past midnight before we reach your brother's clearing," (where we expected to spend the night,) said D——. "I wish, Mr. Moodie, we had followed your advice, and staid at Peterborough. How fares it with you, Mrs. Moodie, and the young ones? It is growing very cold."

We were now in the heart of a dark cedar swamp, and my mind was haunted with visions of wolves and bears; but beyond the long, wild howl of a solitary wolf, no other sound awoke the sepulchral silence of that dismal-looking wood.

"What a gloomy spot," said I to my husband. "In the old country, superstition would people it with ghosts."

"Ghosts! There are no ghosts in Canada!" said Mr. D——. "The country is too new for ghosts. No Canadian is afeard of ghosts. It is only in old countries, like your'n, that are full of sin and wickedness, that people believe in such nonsense. No human habitation has ever been erected in this wood through which you are passing. Until a very few years ago, few white persons had ever passed through it; and the Red Man would not pitch his tent in such a place as this.

Now, ghosts, as I understand the word, are the spirits of bad men, that are not allowed by Providence to rest in their graves, but, for a punishment, are made to haunt the spots where their worst deeds were committed. I don't believe in all this; but, supposing it to be true, bad men must have died here before their spirits could haunt the place. Now, it is more than probable that no person ever ended his days in this forest, so that it would be folly to think of seeing his ghost."

This theory of Mr. D——'s had the merit of originality, and it is not improbable that the utter disbelief in supernatural appearances, which is common to most native-born Canadians, is the result of the same very reasonable mode of arguing. The unpeopled wastes of Canada must present the same aspect to the new settler that the world did to our first parents after their expulsion from the garden of Eden; all the sin which could defile the spot, or haunt it with the association of departed evil, is concentrated in their own persons. Bad spirits cannot be supposed to linger near a place where crime has never been committed. The belief in ghosts, so prevalent in old countries, must first have had its foundation in the consciousness of guilt.

After clearing this low, swampy portion of the wood, with much difficulty, and the frequent application of the axe, to cut away the fallen timber that impeded our progress, our ears were assailed by a low, roaring, rushing sound, as of the falling of waters.

"That is Herriot's Falls," said our guide. "We are within two miles of our destination."

Oh, welcome sound! But those two miles appeared more lengthy than the whole journey. Thick clouds, that threatened a snow-storm, had blotted out the stars, and we continued to grope our way through a narrow, rocky path, upon the edge of the river, in almost total darkness. I now felt the chillness of the midnight hour, and the fatigue of the long journey, with double force, and envied the servant and children, who had been sleeping ever since we left Peterborough. We now descended the steep bank, and prepared to cross the rapids.

Dark as it was, I looked with a feeling of dread upon the foaming waters as they tumbled over their bed of rocks, their white crests flashing, life-like, amid the darkness of the night.

"This is an ugly bridge over such a dangerous place," said D——, as he stood up in the sleigh and urged his tired team across the miserable, insecure log-bridge, where darkness and death raged below, and one false step of his jaded horses would have plunged us into both. I must confess I drew a freer breath when the bridge was crossed, and D—— congratulated us on our safe arrival in Douro.

We now continued our journey along the left bank of the river, but when in sight of Mr. S——'s clearing, a large pine-tree, which had newly fallen across the narrow path, brought the teams to a stand-still. The mighty trunk which had lately formed one of the stately pillars in the sylvan temple of Nature, was of too large dimensions to chop in two with axes; and after half-an-hour's labour, which to me, poor, cold, weary wight! seemed an age, the males of the party abandoned the task in despair. To go round it was impossible; its roots were concealed in an impenetrable wall of cedar-jungle on the right-hand side of the road, and its huge branches hung over the precipitous bank of the river.

We must try and make the horses jump over it," said D——. "We may get an upset, but there is no help for it; we must either make the experiment, or stay here all night, and I am too cold and hungry for that—so here goes." He urged his horses to leap the log; restraining their ardour for a moment as the sleigh rested on the top of the formidable barrier, but so nicely balanced, that the difference of a straw would almost have overturned the heavily-laden vehicle and its helpless inmates. We, however, cleared it in safety. He now stopped, and gave directions to his brother to follow the same plan that he had adopted; but whether the young man had less coolness, or the horses in his team were more difficult to manage, I cannot tell: the sleigh, as it hung poised upon the top of the log, was overturned with a loud crash, and all my household goods and chattels were scattered over the road. Alas, for my crockery and stone china! scarcely one article remained unbroken.

"Never fret about the china," said Moodie; "thank God, the man and the horses are uninjured."

I should have felt more thankful had the crocks been spared too; for, like most of my sex, I had a tender regard for china, and I knew that no fresh supply could be obtained in this part of the world. Leaving his brother to collect the scattered fragments, D—— proceeded on his journey. We left the road, and were winding our way over a steep hill, covered with heaps of brush and fallen timber, and as we reached the top, a light gleamed cheerily from the windows of a log house, and the next moment we were at my brother's door.

I thought my journey was at an end; but here I was doomed to fresh disappointment. His wife was absent on a visit to her friends, and it had been arranged that we were to to stay with my sister, Mrs. T——, and her husband. With all this I was unacquainted; and I was about to quit the sleigh and seek the warmth of the fire when I was told that I had yet further to go. Its cheerful glow was to shed no warmth on me, and, tired as I was, I actually buried my face and wept upon the neck of a hound which Moodie had given to Mr. S——, and which sprang up upon the sleigh to lick my face and hands. This was my first halt in that weary wilderness, where I endured so many bitter years of toil and sorrow. My brother-in-law and his family had retired to rest, but they instantly rose to receive the way-worn travellers; and I never enjoyed more heartily a warm welcome after a long day of intense fatigue, than I did that night of my first sojourn in the backwoods.

## CHAPTER II.

### THE WILDERNESS, AND OUR INDIAN FRIENDS.

THE clouds of the preceding night, instead of dissolving into snow, brought on a rapid thaw. A thaw in the middle of winter is the most disagreeable change that can be imagined. After several weeks of clear, bright, bracing, frosty weather, with a serene atmosphere and cloudless sky, you awake one morning surprised at the change in the temperature; and, upon looking out of the window, behold the woods obscured by a murky haze—not so dense as an English November fog, but more black and lowering—and the heavens shrouded in a uniform covering of leaden-coloured clouds, deepening into a livid indigo at the edge of the horizon. The snow, no longer hard and glittering, has become soft and spongy, and the foot slips into a wet and insidiously-yielding mass at every step. From the roof pours down a continuous stream of water, and the branches of the trees collecting the moisture of the reeking atmosphere, shower it upon the earth from every dripping twig. The cheerless and uncomfortable aspect of things without never fails to produce a corresponding effect upon the minds of those within, and casts such a damp upon the spirits that it appears to destroy for a time all sense of enjoyment. Many persons (and myself among the number) are made aware of the approach of a thunder-storm by an intense pain and weight about the head; and I have heard numbers of

Canadians complain that a thaw always made them feel bilious and heavy, and greatly depressed their animal spirits.

I had a great desire to visit our new location, but when I looked out upon the cheerless waste, I gave up the idea, and contented myself with hoping for a better day on the morrow; but many morrows came and went before a frost again hardened the road sufficiently for me to make the attempt.

The prospect from the windows of my sister's log hut was not very prepossessing. The small lake in front, which formed such a pretty object in summer, now looked like an extensive field covered with snow, hemmed in from the rest of the world by a dark belt of sombre pine-woods. The clearing round the house was very small, and only just reclaimed from the wilderness, and the greater part of it covered with piles of brushwood, to be burned the first dry days of spring. The charred and blackened stumps on the few acres that had been cleared during the preceding year were every thing but picturesque; and I concluded, as I turned, disgusted, from the prospect before me, that there was very little beauty to be found in the backwoods. But I came to this decision during a Canadian thaw, be it remembered, when one is wont to view every object with jaundiced eyes.

Moodie had only been able to secure sixty-six acres of his government grant upon the Upper Kutchawanook Lake, which, being interpreted, means in English, the "Lake of the Waterfalls," a very poetical meaning, which most Indian names have. He had, however, secured a clergy reserve of two hundred acres adjoining; and he afterwards purchased a fine lot, which likewise formed a part of the same block, one hundred acres, for £150.* This was an enormously high price for wild land;

* After a lapse of fifteen years, we have been glad to sell these lots of land, after considerable clearings had been made upon them, for less than they originally cost us.

but the prospect of opening the Trent and Otonabee for the navigation of steamboats and other small craft, was at that period a favourite speculation, and its practicability, and the great advantages to be derived from it, were so widely believed, as to raise the value of the wild lands along these remote waters to an enormous price; and settlers in the vicinity were eager to secure lots, at any sacrifice, along their shores.

Our government grant was upon the lake shore, and Moodie had chosen for the site of his log house a bank that sloped gradually from the edge of the water, until it attained to the dignity of a hill. Along the top of this ridge, the forest-road ran, and midway down the hill, our humble home, already nearly completed, stood, surrounded by the eternal forest. A few trees had been cleared in its immediate vicinity, just sufficient to allow the workmen to proceed, and to prevent the fall of any tree injuring the building, or the danger of its taking fire during the process of burning the fallow.

A neighbour had undertaken to build this rude dwelling by contract, and was to have it ready for us by the first week in the new year. The want of boards to make the divisions in the apartments alone hindered him from fulfilling his contract. These had lately been procured, and the house was to be ready for our reception in the course of a week. Our trunks and baggage had already been conveyed by Mr. D—— hither; and in spite of my sister's kindness and hospitality, I longed to find myself once more settled in a home of my own.

The day after our arrival, I was agreeably surprised by a visit from Monaghan, whom Moodie had once more taken into his service. The poor fellow was delighted that his nurse-child, as he always called little Katie, had not forgotten him, but evinced the most lively satisfaction at the sight of her dark friend.

Early every morning, Moodie went off to the house; and the first fine day, my sister undertook to escort me through the wood, to inspect it. The proposal was joyfully accepted; and although I felt *rather* timid when I found myself with only my female companion in the vast forest, I kept my fears to myself, lest I should be laughed at. This foolish dread of encountering wild beasts in the woods, I never could wholly shake off, even after becoming a constant resident in their gloomy depths, and accustomed to follow the forest-path, alone, or attended with little children, daily. The cracking of an old bough, or the hooting of the owl, was enough to fill me with alarm, and try my strength in a precipitate flight. Often have I stopped and reproached myself for want of faith in the goodness of Providence, and repeated the text, "The wicked are afraid when no man pursueth: but the righteous are as bold as a lion," as if to shame myself into courage. But it would not do; I could not overcome the weakness of the flesh. If I had one of my infants with me, the wish to protect the child from any danger which might beset my path gave me for a time a fictitious courage; but it was like love fighting with despair.

It was in vain that my husband assured me that no person had ever been attacked by wild animals in the woods, that a child might traverse them even at night in safety; whilst I knew that wild animals existed in those woods, I could not believe him, and my fears on this head rather increased than diminished.

The snow had been so greatly decreased by the late thaw, that it had been converted into a coating of ice, which afforded a dangerous and slippery footing. My sister, who had resided for nearly twelve months in the woods, was provided for her walk with Indian moccasins, which rendered her quite independent; but I stumbled at every step. The sun shone brightly, the air was clear and invigorating, and, in spite of the treacherous ground and my foolish fears, I greatly enjoyed my first walk in the woods. Naturally of a cheerful, hopeful disposition, my sister was enthusiastic in her admiration of the woods. She drew such a lively picture of the charms of a summer residence in the forest that I began to feel greatly interested in her descriptions, and to rejoice that we too were to be her near neighbours and dwellers in the woods; and this circumstance not a little reconciled me to the change.

Hoping that my husband would derive an income equal to the one he had parted with from the investment of the price of his commission in the steamboat stock, I felt no dread of want. Our legacy of £700 had afforded us means to purchase land, build our house, and give out a large portion of land to be cleared, and, with a considerable sum of money still in hand, our prospects for the future were in no way discouraging.

When we reached the top of the ridge that overlooked our cot, my sister stopped, and pointed out a large dwelling among the trees. "There, S——," she said, "is your home. When that black cedar swamp is cleared away, that now hides the lake from us, you will have a very pretty view." My conversation with her had quite altered the aspect of the country, and predisposed me to view things in the most favourable light. I found Moodie and Monaghan employed in piling up heaps of bush near the house, which they intended to burn off by hand previous to firing the rest of the fallow, to prevent any risk to the building from fire. The house was made of cedar logs, and presented a superior air of comfort to most dwellings of the same kind. The dimensions were thirty-six feet in length, and thirty-two in breadth, which gave us a nice parlour, a kitchen, and two small bedrooms, which were divided by plank partitions. Pantry or storeroom there was none; some rough shelves in the kitchen, and a deal cupboard in a corner of the parlour, being the extent of our accommodations in that way.

Our servant, Mary Tate, was busy scrubbing out the parlour and bedroom; but the kitchen, and the sleeping-room off it, were still knee-deep in chips, and filled with the carpenter's bench and tools, and all our luggage. Such as it was, it was a palace when compared to Old Satan's log hut, or the miserable cabin we had wintered in during the severe winter of 1833, and I regarded it with complacency as my future home.

While we were standing outside the building, conversing with my husband, a young gentleman, of the name of Morgan, who had lately purchased land in that vicinity, went into the kitchen to light his pipe at the stove, and, with true backwood carelessness, let the hot cinder fall among the dry chips that strewed the floor. A few minutes after, the whole mass was in a blaze, and it was not without great difficulty that Moodie and Mr. R—— succeeded in putting out the fire. Thus were we nearly deprived of our home before we had taken up our abode in it.

The indifference to the danger of fire in a country where most of the dwellings are composed of inflammable materials, is truly astonishing. Accustomed to see enormous fires blazing on every hearth-stone, and to sleep in front of these fires, his bedding often riddled with holes made by hot particles of wood flying out during the night, and igniting beneath his very nose, the sturdy backwoodsman never dreads an enemy in the element that he is used to regard as his best friend. Yet what awful accidents, what ruinous calamities arise, out of this criminal negligence, both to himself and others!

A few days after this adventure, we bade adieu to my sister, and took possession of our new dwelling and commenced "a life in the woods."

The first spring we spent in comparative ease and idleness. Our cows had been left upon our old place during the winter. The ground had to be cleared before it could receive a crop of any kind, and I had little to do but to wander by the lake shore, or among the woods, and amuse myself. These were the halcyon days of the bush.. My husband had purchased a very light cedar canoe, to which he attached a keel and a sail; and most of our leisure hours, directly the snows melted, were spent upon the water.

These fishing and shooting excursions were delightful. The pure beauty of the Canadian water, the sombre but august grandeur of the vast forest that hemmed us in on every side and shut us out from the rest of the world, soon cast a magic spell upon our spirits, and we began to feel charmed with the freedom and solitude around us. Every object was new to us. We felt as if we were the first discoverers of every beautiful flower and stately tree that attracted our attention, and we gave names to fantastic rocks and fairy isles, and raised imaginary houses and bridges on every picturesque spot which we floated past during our aquatic excursions. I learned the use of the paddle, and became quite a proficient in the gentle craft.

It was not long before we received visits from the Indians, a people whose beauty, talents, and good qualities have been somewhat overrated, and invested with a poetical interest which they scarcely deserve. Their honesty and love of truth are the finest traits in characters otherwise dark and unlovely. But these are two God-like attributes, and from them spring all that is generous and ennobling about them.

There never was a people more sensible of kindness, or more grateful for any little act of benevolence exercised to wards them. We met them with confidence; our dealings with them were conducted with the strictest integrity; and they became attached to our persons, and in no single instance ever destroyed the good opinion we entertained of them.

The tribes that occupy the shores of all these inland waters, back of the great lakes, belong to the Chippewa or Missasagua Indians, perhaps the least attractive of all these wild people, both with regard to their physical and mental endowments. The men of this tribe are generally small of stature, with very coarse and repulsive features. The forehead is low and retreating, the observing faculties large, the intellectual ones scarcely developed; the ears large, and standing off from the face; the eyes looking towards the temples, keen, snake-like, and far apart; the cheek-bones prominent; the nose long and flat, the nostrils very round; the jaw-bone projecting, massy, and brutal; the mouth expressing ferocity and sullen determination; the teeth large, even, and dazzilngly white. The mouth of the female differs widely in expression from that of the male; the lips are fuller, the jaw less projecting, and the smile is simple and agreeable. The women are a merry, light-hearted set, and their constant laugh and incessant prattle form a strange contrast to the iron taciturnity of their grim lords.

Now I am upon the subject, I will recapitulate a few traits and sketches of these people, as they came under my own immediate observation.

A dry cedar swamp, not far from the house, by the lake shore, had been their usual place of encampment for many years. The whole block of land was almost entirely covered with maple-trees, and had originally been an Indian sugar-bush. Although the favourite spot had now passed into the hands of strangers, they still frequented the place, to make canoes and baskets, to fish and shoot, and occasionally to follow their old occupation. Scarcely a week passed away without my being visited by the dark strangers; and as my husband never allowed them to eat with the servants, but brought them to his own table, they soon grew friendly and communicative, and would point to every object that attracted their attention, asking a thousand questions as to its use, the material of which it was made, and if we were inclined to exchange it for their commodities? With a large map of Canada, they were infinitely delighted. In a moment they recognized every bay and headland in Ontario, and almost screamed with delight when, following the course of the Trent with their fingers, they came to their own lake.

How eagerly each pointed out the spot to his fellows; how intently their black heads were bent down, and their dark eyes fixed upon the map! What strange, uncouth exclamations of surprise burst from their lips as they rapidly repeated the Indian names for every lake and river on this wonderful piece of paper!

The old chief, Peter Nogan, begged hard for the coveted treasure. He would give "Canoe, venison, duck, fish, for it; and more, by and by."

I felt sorry that I was unable to gratify his wishes; but the map had cost upwards of six dollars, and was daily consulted by my husband, in reference to the names and situations of localities in the neighbourhood.

I had in my possession a curious Japanese sword, which had been given to me by an uncle of Tom Wilson's—a strange gift to a young lady; but it was on account of its curiosity, and had no reference to my warlike propensities. This sword was broad, and three-sided in the blade, and in shape resembled a moving snake. The hilt was formed of a hideous carved image of one of their war-gods; and a more villainous-looking wretch was never conceived by the most distorted imagination. He was represented in a sitting attitude, the eagle's claws, that formed his hands, resting upon his knees; his legs terminated in lion's paws; and his face was a strange compound of beast and bird—the upper part of his person being covered with feathers, the lower with long, shaggy hair. The case of this awful weapon was made of wood, and, in spite of its serpentine form, fitted it exactly. No trace of a join could be found in this scabbard, which was of hard wood, and highly polished.

One of my Indian friends found this sword lying upon the book-shelf, and he hurried to communicate the important discovery to his companions. Moodie was absent, and they brought it to me to demand an explanation of the figure that formed the hilt. I told them that it was a weapon that belonged to a very fierce people who lived in the East, far over the Great Salt Lake; that they were not Christians, as we were, but said their prayers to images made of silver, and gold, and ivory, and wood, and that this was one of them; that before they went into battle they said their prayers to that hideous thing, which they had made with their own hands. The Indians were highly amused by this relation, and passed the sword from one to the other, exclaiming, "A god!—Owgh!—A god!"

But, in spite of these outward demonstrations of contempt, I was sorry to perceive that this circumstance gave the weapon a great value in their eyes, and they regarded it with a sort of mysterious awe.

For several days they continued to visit the house, bringing along with them some fresh companion to look at Mrs. Moodie's *god!*—until, vexed and annoyed by the delight they manifested at the sight of the eagle-beaked monster, I refused to gratify their curiosity, by not producing him again.

The manufacture of the sheath, which had caused me much perplexity, was explained by old Peter in a minute. "'Tis burnt out," he said. "Instrument made like sword—heat red-hot—burnt through—polished outside."

Had I demanded a whole fleet of canoes for my Japanese sword, I am certain they would have agreed to the bargain. The Indian possesses great taste, which is displayed in the carving of his paddles, in the shape of his canoes, in the elegance and symmetry of his bows, in the cut of his leggings and moccasins, the sheath of his hunting-knife, and in all the little ornaments in which he delights. It is almost impossible for a settler to imitate to perfection an Indian's cherry-wood paddle. My husband made very creditable attempts, but still there was something wanting—the elegance of the Indian finish was not there. If you show them a good print, they invariably point out the most natural and the best-executed figure in the group. They are particularly delighted with pictures, examine them long and carefully, and seem to feel an artist-like pleasure in observing the effect produced by light and shade.

I had been showing John Nogan, the eldest son of old Peter, some beautiful coloured engravings of celebrated females; and to my astonishment he pounced upon the best, and grunted out his admiration in the most approved Indian fashion. After having looked for a long time at all the pictures very attentively, he took his dog Sancho upon his knee, and showed him the pictures, with as much gravity as if the animal really could have shared in his pleasure. The vanity of these grave men is highly amusing. They seem perfectly unconscious of it themselves; and it is exhibited in the most childlike manner.

Peter and his son John were taking tea with us, when we were joined by my brother, Mr. S——. The latter was giving us an account of the marriage of Peter Jones, the celebrated Indian preacher.

"I cannot think," he said, "how any lady of property and education could marry such a man as Jones. Why, he's as ugly as Peter here."

This was said, not with any idea of insulting the red-skin on the score of his beauty, of which he possessed not the smallest particle, but in total forgetfulness that our guest understood English. Never shall I forget the red flash of that fierce, dark eye as it glared upon my unconscious brother. I would not have received such a fiery glance for all the wealth that Peter Jones obtained with his Saxon bride. John Nogan was highly amused by his father's indignation. He hid his face behind the chief; and though he kept perfectly still, his whole frame was convulsed with suppressed laughter.

A plainer human being than poor Peter could scarcely be imagined; yet he certainly deemed himself handsome. I am inclined to think that their ideas of personal beauty differ very widely from ours. Tom Nogan, the chief's brother, had a very large, fat, ugly squaw for his wife. She was a mountain of tawny flesh; and, but for the innocent, good-natured expression which, like a bright sunbeam penetrating a swarthy cloud, spread all around a kindly glow, she might have been termed hideous.

This woman they considered very handsome, calling her "a fine squaw—clever squaw—a much good woman;" though in what her superiority consisted, I never could discover, often as I visited the wigwam. She was very dirty, and appeared quite indifferent to the claims of common decency (in the disposal of the few filthy rags that covered her). She was, however, very expert in all Indian craft. No Jew could drive a better bargain than Mrs. Tom; and her urchins, of whom she was the happy mother of five or six, were as cunning and avaricious as herself. One day she visited me, bringing along with her a very pretty covered basket for sale. I asked her what she wanted for it, but could obtain from her no satisfactory answer. I showed her a small piece of silver. She shook her head. I tempted her with pork and flour, but she required neither. I had just given up the idea of dealing with her, in despair, when she suddenly seized upon me, and, lifting up my gown, pointed exultingly to my quilted petticoat, clapping her hands, and laughing immoderately.

Another time she led me all over the house, to show me what she wanted in exchange for *basket*. My patience was well nigh exhausted in following her from place to place, in her attempt to discover the coveted article, when, hanging upon a peg in my chamber, she espied a pair of trowsers belonging to my husband's logging-suit. The riddle was solved. With a joyful cry she pointed to them, exclaiming "Take basket.—Give them!" It was with no small difficulty that I rescued the indispensables from her grasp.

From this woman I learned a story of Indian coolness and courage which made a deep impression on my mind. One of their squaws, a near relation of her own, had accompanied her husband on a hunting expedition into the forest. He had been very successful, and having killed more deer than they could well carry home, he went to the house of a white man to dispose of some of it, leaving the squaw to take care of the rest until his return. She sat carelessly upon the log with his hunting-knife in her hand, when she heard the breaking of branches near her, and, turning round, beheld a great bear only a few paces from her.

It was too late to retreat; and seeing that the animal was very hungry, and determined to come to close quarters, she rose, and placed her back against a small tree, holding her knife close to her breast, and in a straight line with the bear.

The shaggy monster came on. She remained motionless, her eyes steadily fixed upon her enemy, and as his huge arms closed around her, she slowly drove the knife into his heart. The bear uttered a hideous cry, and sank dead at her feet. When the Indian returned, he found the courageous woman taking the skin from the carcass of the formidable brute.

The wolf they hold in great contempt, and scarcely deign to consider him as an enemy. Peter Nogan assured me that he never was near enough to one in his life to shoot it; that, except in large companies, and when greatly pressed by hunger, they rarely attack men. They hold the lynx, or wolverine, in much dread, as they often spring from trees upon their prey, fastening upon the throat with their sharp teeth and claws, from which a person in the dark could scarcely free himself without first receiving a dangerous wound. The cry of this animal is very terrifying, resembling the shrieks of a human creature in mortal agony.

My husband was anxious to collect some of the native Indian airs, as they all sing well, and have a fine ear for music, but all his efforts proved abortive. "John," he said to young Nogan (who played very creditably on the flute, and had just concluded the popular air of "Sweet Home"), "cannot you play me one of your own songs?"

"Yes,—but no good."

"Leave me to be the judge of that. Cannot you give me a war-song?"

"Yes,—but no good," with an ominous shake of the head.

"A hunting-song?"

"No fit for white man,"—with an air of contempt.—"No good, no good!"

"Do, John, sing us a love-song," said I, laughing, "if you have such a thing in your language."

"Oh! much love-song—very much—bad—bad—no good

for Christian man. Indian song no good for white ears." This was very tantalizing, as their songs sounded very sweetly from the lips of their squaws, and I had a great desire and curiosity to get some of them rendered into English.

To my husband they gave the name of "the musician," but I have forgotten the Indian word. It signified the maker of sweet sounds. They listened with intense delight to the notes of his flute, maintained a breathless silence during the performance; their dark eyes flashing in fierce light at a martial strain, or softening with the plaintive and tender.

The affection of Indian parents to their children, and the deference which they pay to the aged, is a beautiful and touching trait in their character.

One extremely cold, wintry day, as I was huddled with my little ones over the stove, the door softly unclosed, and the moccasined foot of an Indian crossed the floor. I raised my head, for I was too much accustomed to their sudden appearance at any hour to feel alarmed, and perceived a tall woman standing silently and respectfully before me, wrapped in a large blanket. The moment she caught my eye she dropped the folds of her covering from around her, and laid at my feet the attenuated figure of a boy, about twelve years of age, who was in the last stage of consumption.

"Papouse die," she said, mournfully, clasping her hands against her breast, and looking down upon the suffering lad with the most heartfelt expression of maternal love, while large tears trickled down her dark face. "Moodie's squaw save papouse—poor Indian woman much glad."

Her child was beyond all human aid. I looked anxiously upon him, and knew, by the pinched-up features and purple hue of his wasted cheek, that he had not many hours to live. I could only answer with tears her agonizing appeal to my skill.

"Try and save him! All die but him." (She held up five of her fingers.) "Brought him all the way from Mutta Lake* upon my back, for white squaw to cure."

"I cannot cure him, my poor friend. He is in God's care; in a few hours he will be with Him."

The child was seized with a dreadful fit of coughing, which I expected every moment would terminate his frail existence. I gave him a tea-spoonful of currant-jelly, which he took with avidity, but could not retain a moment on his stomach.

"Papouse die," murmured the poor woman; "alone—alone! No papouse; the mother all alone."

She began re-adjusting the poor sufferer in her blanket. I got her some food, and begged her to stay and rest herself; but she was too much distressed to eat, and too restless to remain. She said little, but her face expressed the keenest anguish; she took up her mournful load, pressed for a moment his wasted, burning hand in hers, and left the room.

My heart followed her a long way on her melancholy journey. Think what this woman's love must have been for that dying son, when she had carried a lad of his age six miles, through the deep snow, upon her back, on such a day, in the hope of my being able to do him some good. Poor heart-broken mother! I learned from Joe Muskrat's squaw some days after that the boy died a few minutes after Elizabeth Iron, his mother, got home.

They never forget any little act of kindness. One cold night, late in the fall, my hospitality was demanded by six squaws, and puzzled I was how to accommodate them all. I at last determined to give them the use of the parlour floor during the night. Among these women there was one very old, whose hair was as white as snow. She was the only gray-

* Mud Lake, or Lake *Shemong*, in Indian.

haired Indian I ever saw, and on that account I regarded her with peculiar interest. I knew that she was the wife of a chief, by the scarlet embroidered leggings, which only the wives and daughters of chiefs are allowed to wear. The old squaw had a very pleasing countenance, but I tried in vain to draw her into conversation. She evidently did not understand me; and the Muskrat squaw, and Betty Cow, were laughing at my attempts to draw her out. I administered supper to them with my own hands, and after I had satisfied their wants, (which is no very easy task, for they have great appetites,) I told our servant to bring in several spare mattresses and blankets for their use. "Now mind, Jenny, and give the old squaw the best bed," I said; "the others are young and can put up with a little inconvenience."

The old Indian glanced at me with her keen, bright eye; but I had no idea that she comprehended what I said. Some weeks after this, as I was sweeping over my parlour floor, a slight tap drew me to the door. On opening it I perceived the old squaw, who immediately slipped into my hand a set of beautifully-embroidered bark trays, fitting one within the other, and exhibiting the very best sample of the porcupine-quill work. While I stood wondering what this might mean, the good old creature fell upon my neck, and kissing me, exclaimed, "You remember old squaw—make her comfortable! Old squaw no forget you. Keep them for her sake," and before I could detain her she ran down the hill with a swiftness which seemed to bid defiance to years. I never saw this interesting Indian again, and I concluded that she died during the winter, for she must have been of a great age.

A friend was staying with us, who wished much to obtain a likeness of Old Peter. I promised to try and make a sketch of the old man the next time he paid us a visit. That very afternoon he brought us some ducks in exchange for pork, and Moodie asked him to stay and take a glass of whiskey with him and his friend Mr. K——. The old man had arrayed himself in a new blanket-coat, bound with red, and the seams all decorated with the same gay material. His leggings and moccasins were new, and elaborately fringed; and, to cap the climax of the whole, he had a blue cloth conical cap upon his head, ornamented with a deer's tail dyed blue, and several cock's feathers. He was evidently very much taken up with the magnificence of his own appearance, for he often glanced at himself in a small shaving-glass that hung opposite, with a look of grave satisfaction. Sitting apart that I might not attract his observation, I got a tolerably faithful likeness of the old man, which, after slightly colouring, to show more plainly his Indian finery, I quietly handed over to Mr. K——. Sly as I thought myself, my occupation and the object of it had not escaped the keen eye of the old man. He rose, came behind Mr. K——'s chair, and regarded the picture with a most affectionate eye. I was afraid that he would be angry at the liberty I had taken. No such thing! He was as pleased as Punch.

"That Peter?" he grunted. "Give me—put up in wigwam—make dog too! Owgh! owgh!" and he rubbed his hands together, and chuckled with delight. Mr. K—— had some difficulty in coaxing the picture from the old chief; so pleased was he with this rude representation of himself. He pointed to every particular article of his dress, and dwelt with peculiar glee on the cap and blue deer's tail.

A few days after this, I was painting a beautiful little snow-bird, that our man had shot out of a large flock that alighted near the door. I was so intent upon my task, to which I was putting the finishing strokes, that I did not observe the stealthy entrance (for they all walk like cats) of a stern-looking red man, till a slender, dark hand was extended over my paper to grasp the dead bird from which I was copying, and which as rapidly transferred it to the side of the painted one, accompanying the act with the deep guttural note of approbation, the unmusical, savage " Owgh."

My guest then seated himself with the utmost gravity in a rocking-chair, directly fronting me, and made the modest demand that I should paint a likeness of him, after the following quaint fashion:

" Moodie's squaw know much—make Peter Nogan toder day on papare—make Jacob to-day—Jacob young—great hunter—give much duck—venison—to squaw."

Although I felt rather afraid of my fierce-looking visitor, I could scarcely keep my gravity; there was such an air of pompous self-approbation about the Indian, such a sublime look of conceit in his grave vanity.

" Moodie's squaw cannot do every thing; she cannot paint young men," said I, rising, and putting away my drawing materials, upon which he kept his eye intently fixed, with a hungry, avaricious expression. I thought it best to place the coveted objects beyond his reach. After sitting for some time, and watching all my movements, he withdrew, with a sullen, disappointed air. This man was handsome, but his expression was vile. Though he often came to the house, I never could reconcile myself to his countenance.

Late one very dark, stormy night, three Indians begged to be allowed to sleep by the kitchen stove. The maid was frightened out of her wits at the sight of these strangers, who were Mohawks from the Indian woods upon the Bay of Quinté, and they brought along with them a horse and cutter. The night was so stormy, that, after consulting our man—Jacob Faithful, as we usually called him—I consented to grant their petition, although they were quite strangers, and taller and fiercer-looking than our friends the Missasaguas.

I was putting my children to bed, when the girl came rushing in, out of breath. "The Lord preserve us, madam, if one of these wild men has not pulled off his trowsers, and is a-sitting mending them behind the stove! and what shall I do?"

"Do?—why, stay with me, and leave the poor fellow to finish his work."

The simple girl had never once thought of this plan of pacifying her outraged sense of propriety.

Their sense of hearing is so acute that they can distinguish sounds at an incredible distance, which cannot be detected by a European at all. I myself witnessed a singular exemplification of this fact. It was mid-winter; the Indians had pitched their tent, or wigwam, as usual, in our swamp. All the males were absent on a hunting expedition up the country, and had left two women behind to take care of the camp and its contents, Mrs. Tom Nogan and her children, and Susan Moore, a young girl of fifteen, and the only truly beautiful squaw I ever saw. There was something interesting about this girl's history, as well as her appearance. Her father had been drowned during a sudden hurricane, which swamped his canoe on Stony Lake; and the mother, who witnessed the accident from the shore, and was near her confinement with this child, boldly swam out to his assistance. She reached the spot where he sank, and even succeeded in recovering the body; but it was too late; the man was dead.

The soul of an Indian that has been drowned is reckoned accursed, and he is never permitted to join his tribe on the happy hunting-grounds, but his spirit haunts the lake or river in which he lost his life. His body is buried on some lonely island, which the Indians never pass without leaving a small portion of food, tobacco, or ammunition, to supply his wants; but he is never interred with the rest of his people. His children are considered unlucky, and few willingly unite themselves to the females of the family, lest a portion of the father's curse should be visited on them.

The orphan Indian girl generally kept aloof from the rest, and seemed so lonely and companionless, that she soon attracted my attention and sympathy, and a hearty feeling of good-will sprang up between us. Her features were small and regular, her face oval, and her large, dark, loving eyes were full of tenderness and sensibility, but as bright and shy as those of the deer. A rich vermilion glow burnt upon her olive cheek and lips, and set off the dazzling whiteness of her even and pearly teeth. She was small of stature, with delicate little hands and feet, and her figure was elastic and graceful. She was a beautiful child of nature, and her Indian name signified "the voice of angry waters." Poor girl, she had been a child of grief and tears from her birth! Her mother was a Mohawk, from whom she, in all probability, derived her superior personal attractions; for they are very far before the Missasaguas in this respect.

My friend and neighbour, Emilia S——, the wife of a naval officer, who lived about a mile distant from me, through the bush, had come to spend the day with me; and hearing that the Indians were in the swamp, and the men away, we determined to take a few trifles to the camp, in the way of presents, and spend an hour in chatting with the squaws.

What a beautiful moonlight night it was, as light as day! —the great forest sleeping tranquilly beneath the cloudless heavens—not a sound to disturb the deep repose of nature but the whispering of the breeze, which, during the most profound calm, creeps through the lofty pine tops. We bounded down the steep bank to the lake shore. Life is a blessing, a precious boon indeed, in such an hour, and we felt happy in the mere consciousness of existence—the glorious privilege of pouring out the silent adoration of the heart to the Great Father in his universal temple.

On entering the wigwam, which stood within a few yards of the clearing, in the middle of a thick group of cedars, we found Mrs. Tom alone with her elvish children, seated before the great fire that burned in the centre of the camp; she was busy boiling some bark in an iron spider. The little boys, in red flannel shirts, which were their only covering, were tormenting a puppy, which seemed to take their pinching and pommelling in good part, for it neither attempted to bark nor to bite, but like the eels in the story, submitted to the infliction because it was used to it. Mrs. Tom greeted us with a grin of pleasure, and motioned us to sit down upon a buffalo skin, which, with a courtesy so natural to the Indians, she had placed near her for our accommodation.

"You are all alone," said I, glancing round the camp.

"Ye'es; Indian away hunting—Upper Lakes. Come home with much deer."

"And Susan, where is she?"

"By and by," (meaning that she was coming). "Gone to fetch water—ice thick—chop with axe—take long time."

As she ceased speaking, the old blanket that formed the door of the tent was withdrawn, and the girl, bearing two pails of water, stood in the open space, in the white moonlight. The glow of the fire streamed upon her dark, floating locks, danced in the black, glistening eye, and gave a deeper blush to the olive cheek! She would have made a beautiful picture; Sir Joshua Reynolds would have rejoiced in such a model—so simply graceful and unaffected, the very *beau idéal* of savage life and unadorned nature. A smile of recognition passed between us. She put down her burden beside Mrs. Tom, and noiselessly glided to her seat.

We had scarcely exchanged a few words with our favourite, when the old squaw, placing her hand against her ear, exclaimed, "Whist! whist!"

"What is it?" cried Emilia and I, starting to our feet. "Is there any danger?"

"A deer—a deer—in bush!" whispered the squaw, seizing a rifle that stood in a corner. "I hear sticks crack—a great way off. Stay here!"

A great way off the animal must have been, for though Emilia and I listened at the open door, an advantage which the squaw did not enjoy, we could not hear the least sound: all seemed still as death. The squaw whistled to an old hound, and went out.

"Did you hear any thing, Susan?"

She smiled, and nodded.

"Listen; the dog has found the track."

The next moment the discharge of a rifle, and the deep baying of the dog, woke up the sleeping echoes of the woods; and the girl started off to help the old squaw to bring in the game that she had shot.

The Indians are great imitators, and possess a nice tact in adopting the customs and manners of those with whom they associate. An Indian is Nature's gentleman—never familiar, coarse, or vulgar. If he take a meal with you, he waits to see how you make use of the implements on the table, and the manner in which you eat, which he imitates with a grave decorum, as if he had been accustomed to the same usages from childhood. He never attempts to help himself, or demand more food, but waits patiently until you perceive what he requires. I was perfectly astonished at this innate politeness, for it seems natural to all the Indians with whom I have had any dealings.

There was one old Indian, who belonged to a distant settlement, and only visited our lakes occasionally on hunting parties. He was a strange, eccentric, merry old fellow, with a skin like red mahogany, and a wiry, sinewy frame, that looked as if it could bid defiance to every change of temperature. Old Snow-storm, for such was his significant name, was rather too fond of the whiskey-bottle, and when he had taken a drop too much, he became an unmanageable wild beast. He had a great fancy for my husband, and never visited the other Indians without extending the same favour to us. Once upon a time, he broke the nipple of his gun; and Moodie repaired the injury for him by fixing a new one in its place, which little kindness quite won the heart of the old man, and he never came to see us without bringing an offering of fish, ducks, partridges, or venison, to show his gratitude.

One warm September day, he made his appearance bareheaded, as usual, and carrying in his hand a great checked bundle.

"Fond of grapes?" said he, putting the said bundle into my hands. "Fine grapes—brought them from island, for my friend's squaw and papouses."

Glad of the donation, which I considered quite a prize, I hastened into the kitchen to untie the grapes and put them into a dish. But imagine my disappointment, when I found them wrapped up in a soiled shirt, only recently taken from the back of the owner. I called Moodie, and begged him to return Snow-storm his garment, and to thank him for the grapes.

The mischievous creature was highly diverted with the circumstance, and laughed immoderately.

"Snow-storm," said he, "Mrs. Moodie and the children are obliged to you for your kindness in bringing them the grapes; but how came you to tie them up in a dirty shirt?"

"Dirty!" cried the old man, astonished that we should object to the fruit on that score. "It ought to be clean; it has been washed often enough. Owgh! You see, Moodie," he continued, "I have no hat—never wear hat—want no shade to my eyes—love the sun—see all around me—up and down —much better widout hat. Could not put grapes in hat— blanket-coat too large, crush fruit, juice run out. I had noting but my shirt, so I takes off shirt, and brings grape safe over the water on my back. Papouse no care for dirty shirt; their *lee-tel bellies have no eyes*."

In spite of this eloquent harangue, I could not bring myself to use the grapes, ripe and tempting as they looked, or give them to the children. Mr. W—— and his wife happening to step in at that moment, fell into such an ecstacy at the sight of the grapes, that, as they were perfectly unacquainted with the circumstance of the shirt, I very *generously* gratified their wishes by presenting them with the contents of the large dish; and they never ate a bit less sweet for the novel mode in which they were conveyed to me!

The Indians, under their quiet exterior, possess a deal of humour. They have significant names for every thing, and a nickname for every one, and some of the latter are laughably appropriate. A fat, pompous, ostentatious settler in our neighbourhood they called *Muckakee*, "the bull-frog." Another, rather a fine young man, but with a very red face, they named *Segoskee*, "the rising sun." Mr. Wood, who had a farm above ours, was a remarkably slender young man, and to him they gave the appellation of *Metiz*, "thin stick." A woman, that occasionally worked for me, had a disagreeable squint; she was known in Indian by the name of *Sachábó*, "cross-eye." A gentleman with a very large nose was *Choojas*, "big, or ugly nose." My little Addie, who was a fair, lovely creature, they viewed with great approbation, and called *Anoonk*, "a star;" while the rosy Katie was *Nogesigook*, "the northern lights." As to me, I was *Nonocosiqui*, a "humming-bird;" a ridiculous name for a tall woman, but it had reference to the delight I took in painting birds. My friend, Emilia, was "blue cloud;" my little Donald, "frozen face;" young C——, "the red-headed woodpecker," from the colour of his hair; my brother, *Chippewa*, and "the bald-headed eagle." He was an especial favourite among them.

The Indians are often made a prey of and cheated by the unprincipled settlers, who think it no crime to overreach a red skin. One anecdote will fully illustrate this fact. A young squaw, who was near becoming a mother, stopped at a Smith-town settler's house to rest herself. The woman of the house, who was Irish, was peeling for dinner some large white turnips, which her husband had grown in their garden. The Indian had never seen a turnip before, and the appearance of the firm, white, juicy root gave her such a keen craving to taste it that she very earnestly begged for a small piece to eat. She had purchased at Peterborough a large stone-china bowl, of a very handsome pattern, (or, perhaps, got it at the store in exchange for a *basket*,) the worth of which might be half-a-dollar. If the poor squaw longed for the turnip, the value of which could scarcely reach a copper, the covetous European had fixed as longing a glance upon the china bowl, and she was determined to gratify her avaricious desire and obtain it on the most easy terms. She told the squaw, with some disdain, that her man did not grow turnips to give away to "Injuns," but she would sell her one. The squaw offered her four coppers, all the change she had about her. This the woman refused with contempt. She then proffered a basket; but that was not sufficient; nothing would satisfy her but the bowl. The Indian demurred; but opposition had only increased her craving for the turnip in a tenfold degree; and, after a short mental struggle, in which the animal propensity overcame the warnings of prudence, the squaw gave up the bowl, and received in return *one turnip!* The daughter of this woman told me this anecdote of her mother as a very clever thing. What ideas some people have of moral justice!

I have said before that the Indian never forgets a kindness. We had a thousand proofs of this, when, overtaken by misfortune, and withering beneath the iron grasp of poverty, we could scarcely obtain bread for ourselves and our little ones; then it was that the truth of the Eastern proverb was brought home to our hearts, and the goodness of God fully manifested towards us, "Cast thy bread upon the waters, and thou shalt find it after many days." During better times we had treated these poor savages with kindness and liberality, and when dearer friends looked coldly upon us they never forsook us. For many a good meal I have been indebted to them, when I had nothing to give in return, when the pantry was empty, and "the hearth-stone growing cold," as they term the want of provisions to cook at it. And their delicacy in conferring these favours was not the least admirable part of their conduct. John Nogan, who was much attached to us, would bring a fine bunch of ducks, and drop them at my feet "for the papouse," or leave a large muskinonge on the sill of the door, or place a quarter of venison just within it, and slip away without saying a word, thinking that receiving a present from a poor Indian might hurt our feelings, and he would spare us the mortification of returning thanks.

When an Indian loses one of his children, he must keep a strict fast for three days, abstaining from food of any kind. A hunter, of the name of Young, told me a curious story of their rigid observance of this strange rite.

"They had a chief," he said, "a few years ago, whom they called 'Handsome Jack'—whether in derision, I cannot tell, for he was one of the ugliest Indians I ever saw. The scarlet fever got into the camp—a terrible disease in this country, and doubly terrible to those poor creatures who don't know how to treat it. His eldest daughter died. The chief had fasted two days when I met him in the bush. I did not know what had happened, but I opened my wallet, for I was on a hunting expedition, and offered him some bread and dried venison. He looked at me reproachfully.

"'Do white men eat bread the first night their papouse is laid in the earth?'

"I then knew the cause of his depression, and left him."

On the night of the second day of his fast another child died of the fever. He had now to accomplish three more days without tasting food. It was too much even for an Indian. On the evening of the fourth, he was so pressed by ravenous hunger, that he stole into the woods, caught a bull-frog, and devoured it alive. He imagined himself alone, but one of his people, suspecting his intention, had followed him, unperceived, to the bush. The act he had just committed was a hideous crime in their eyes, and in a few minutes the camp was in an uproar. The chief fled for protection to Young's house. When the hunter demanded the cause of his alarm, he gave for answer, "There are plenty of flies at my house. To avoid their stings I came to you."

It required all the eloquence of Mr. Young, who enjoyed much popularity among them, to reconcile the rebellious tribe to their chief.

They are very skilful in their treatment of wounds, and many diseases. Their knowledge of the medicinal qualities of their plants and herbs is very great. They make excellent poultices from the bark of the bass and the slippery-elm. They use several native plants in their dyeing of baskets and porcupine quills. The inner bark of the swamp-alder, simply boiled in water, makes a beautiful red. From the root of the black briony they obtain a fine salve for sores, and extract a rich yellow dye. The inner bark of the root of the sumach, roasted, and reduced to powder, is a good remedy for the ague; a tea-spoonful given between the hot and cold fit. They scrape the fine white powder from the large fungus that grows upon the bark of the pine into whiskey, and take it for violent pains in the stomach. The taste of this powder strongly reminded me of quinine.

I have read much of the excellence of Indian cookery, but I never could bring myself to taste any thing prepared in their dirty wigwams. I remember being highly amused in watching the preparation of a mess, which might have been called the Indian hotch-potch. It consisted of a strange mixture of fish, flesh, and flowl, all boiled together in the same vessel. Ducks, partridges, muskinonge, venison, and muskrats, formed a part of this delectable compound. These were literally smothered in onions, potatoes, and turnips, which they had procured from me. They very hospitably offered me a dishful of the odious mixture, which the odour of the muskrats rendered every thing but savoury; but I declined, simply stating that I was not hungry. My little boy tasted it, but quickly left the camp to conceal the effect it produced upon him.

Their method of broiling fish, however, is excellent. They take a fish, just fresh out of the water, cut out the entrails, and, without removing the scales, wash it clean, dry it in a cloth, or in grease, and cover it all over with clear hot ashes. When the flesh will part from the bone, they draw it out of the ashes, strip off the skin, and it is fit for the table of the most fastidious epicure.

The deplorable want of chastity that exists among the Indian women of this tribe seems to have been more the result of their intercourse with the settlers in the country than from any previous disposition to this vice. The jealousy of their husbands has often been exercised in a terrible manner against the offending squaws; but this has not happened of late years. The men wink at these derelictions in their wives, and share with them the price of their shame.

The mixture of European blood adds greatly to the physical beauty of the half-race, but produces a sad falling off from the original integrity of the Indian character. The half-caste is generally a lying, vicious rogue, possessing the worst qualities of both parents in an eminent degree. We have many of these half-Indians in the penitentiary, for crimes of the blackest dye.

The skill of the Indian in procuring his game, either by land or water, has been too well described by better writers than I could ever hope to be, to need any illustration from my pen, and I will close this long chapter with a droll anecdote which is told of a gentleman in this neighbourhood.

The early loss of his hair obliged Mr. —— to procure the substitute of a wig. This was such a good imitation of nature, that none but his intimate friends and neighbours were aware of the fact. It happened that he had had some quarrel with an Indian, which had to be settled in one of the petty courts. The case was decided in favour of Mr. ——, which so aggrieved the savage, who considered himself the injured party, that he sprang upon him with a furious yell, tomahawk in hand, with the intention of depriving him of his scalp. He twisted his hand in the locks which adorned the cranium of his adversary, when—horror of horrors!—the treacherous wig came off in his hand, "Owgh! owgh!" exclaimed the affrighted savage, flinging it from him, and rushing from the court as if he had been bitten by a rattlesnake. His sudden exit was followed by peals of laughter from the crowd, while Mr. —— coolly picked up his wig, and dryly remarked that it had saved his head.

## CHAPTER III.

### BURNING THE FALLOW.

IT is not my intention to give a regular history of our resi dence in the bush, but merely to present to my readers such events as may serve to illustrate a life in the woods.

The winter and spring of 1834 had passed away. The latter was uncommonly cold and backward; so much so that we had a very heavy fall of snow upon the 14th and 15th of May, and several gentlemen drove down to Cobourg in a sleigh, the snow lying upon the ground to the depth of several inches.

A late, cold spring in Canada is generally succeeded by a burning, hot summer; and the summer of '34 was the hottest I ever remember. No rain fell upon the earth for many weeks, till nature drooped and withered beneath one bright blaze of sunlight; and the ague and fever in the woods, and the cholera in the large towns and cities, spread death and sickness through the country.

Moodie had made during the winter a large clearing of twenty acres around the house. The progress of the workmen had been watched by me with the keenest interest. Every tree that reached the ground opened a wider gap in the dark wood, giving us a broader ray of light and a clearer glimpse of the blue sky. But when the dark cedar swamp fronting the house fell beneath the strokes of the axe, and we got a first view of the lake, my joy was complete; a new and beautiful object was now constantly before me, which gave me the greatest pleasure. By night and day, in sunshine or in storm, water is always the most sublime feature in a landscape, and no view can be truly grand in which it is wanting. From a child, it always had the most powerful effect upon my mind, from the great ocean rolling in majesty, to the tinkling forest rill, hidden by the flowers and rushes along its banks. Half the solitude of my forest home vanished when the lake unveiled its bright face to the blue heavens, and I saw sun and moon and stars and waving trees reflected there. I would sit for hours at the window as the shades of evening deepened round me, watching the massy foliage of the forests pictured in the waters, till fancy transported me back to England, and the songs of birds and the lowing of cattle were sounding in my ears. It was long, very long, before I could discipline my mind to learn and practise all the menial employments which are necessary in a good settler's wife.

The total absence of trees about the doors in all new settlements had always puzzled me, in a country where the intense heat of summer seems to demand all the shade that can be procured. My husband had left several beautiful rock-elms (the most picturesque tree in the country) near our dwelling, but, alas! the first high gale prostrated all my fine trees, and left our log cottage entirely exposed to the fierce rays of the sun. The confusion of an uncleared fallow spread around us on every side. Huge trunks of trees and piles of brush gave a littered and uncomfortable appearance to the locality, and as the weather had been very dry for some weeks, I heard my husband daily talking with his choppers as to the expediency of firing the fallow. They still urged him to wait a little longer, until he could get a good breeze to carry the fire well through the brush.

Business called him suddenly to Toronto, but he left a

strict charge with old Thomas and his sons, who were engaged in the job, by no means to attempt to burn it off till he returned, as he wished to be upon the premises himself, in case of any danger. He had previously burnt all the heaps immediately about the doors. While he was absent, old Thomas and his second son fell sick with the ague, and went home to their own township, leaving John, a surly, obstinate young man, in charge of the shanty, where they slept, and kept their tools and provisions. Monaghan I had sent to fetch up my three cows, as the children were languishing for milk, and Mary and I remained alone in the house with the little ones. The day was sultry, and towards noon a strong wind sprang up that roared in the pine tops like the dashing of distant billows, but without in the least degree abating the heat. The children were lying listlessly upon the floor for coolness, and the girl and I were finishing sun-bonnets, when Mary suddenly exclaimed, "Bless us, mistress, what a smoke!" I ran immediately to the door, but was not able to distinguish ten yards before me. The swamp immediately below us was on fire, and the heavy wind was driving a dense black cloud of smoke directly towards us.

"What can this mean?" I cried, "Who can have set fire to the fallow?"

As I ceased speaking, John Thomas stood pale and trembling before me. "John, what is the meaning of this fire?"

"Oh, ma'am, I hope you will forgive me; it was I set fire to it, and I would give all I have in the world if I had not done it."

"What is the danger?"

"Oh, I'm terribly afeard that we shall all be burnt up," said the fellow, beginning to whimper.

"Why did you run such a risk, and your master from nome. and no one on the place to render the least assistance?"

"I did it for the best," blubbered the lad. "What shall we do?"

"Why, we must get out of it as fast as we can, and leave the house to its fate."

"We can't get out," said the man, in a low, hollow tone, which seemed the concentration of fear; "I would have got out of it if I could; but just step to the back door, ma'am, and see."

I had not felt the least alarm up to this minute; I had never seen a fallow burnt, but I had heard of it as a thing of such common occurrence that I had never connected with it any idea of danger. Judge then, my surprise, my horror, when, on going to the back door, I saw that the fellow, to make sure of his work, had fired the field in fifty different places. Behind, before, on every side, we were surrounded by a wall of fire, burning furiously within a hundred yards of us, and cutting off all possibility of retreat; for could we have found an opening through the burning heaps, we could not have seen our way through the dense canopy of smoke; and, buried as we were in the heart of the forest, no one could discover our situation till we were beyond the reach of help. I closed the door, and went back to the parlour. Fear was knocking loudly at my heart, for our utter helplessness annihilated all hope of being able to effect our escape—I felt stupefied. The girl sat upon the floor by the children, who, unconscious of the peril that hung over them, had both fallen asleep. She was silently weeping; while the fool who had caused the mischief was crying aloud.

A strange calm succeeded my first alarm; tears and lamentations were useless; a horrible death was impending over us, and yet I could not believe that we were to die. I sat down upon the step of the door, and watched the awful scene in silence. The fire was raging in the cedar swamp, immediately below the ridge on which the house stood, and it presented a spectacle truly appalling. From out the dense folds of a canopy of black smoke, the blackest I ever saw, leaped up continually red forks of lurid flame as high as the tree tops, igniting the branches of a group of tall pines that had been left standing for sun-logs. A deep gloom blotted out the heavens from our sight. The air was filled with fiery particles, which floated even to the door-step—while the crackling and roaring of the flames might have been heard at a great distance. Could we have reached the lake shore, where several canoes were moored at the landing, by launching out into the water we should have been in perfect safety; but, to attain this object, it was necessary to pass through this mimic hell; and not a bird could have flown over it with unscorched wings. There was no hope in that quarter, for, could we have escaped the flames, we should have been blinded and choked by the thick, black, resinous smoke. The fierce wind drove the flames at the sides and back of the house up the clearing; and our passage to the road, or to the forest, on the right and left, was entirely obstructed by a sea of flames. Our only ark of safety was the house, so long as it remained untouched by the consuming element. I turned to young Thomas, and asked him, how long he thought that would be.

"When the fire clears this little ridge in front, ma'am. The Lord have mercy upon us, then, or we must all go!"

"Cannot *you*, John, try and make your escape, and see what can be done for us and the poor children?"

My eye fell upon the sleeping angels, locked peacefully in each other's arms, and my tears flowed for the first time. Mary, the servant-girl, looked piteously up in my face. The good, faithful creature had not uttered one word of complaint, but now she faltered forth,

"The dear, precious lambs!—Oh! such a death!"

I threw myself down upon the floor beside them, and pressed them alternately to my heart, while inwardly I thanked God that they were asleep, unconscious of danger, and unable by their childish cries to distract our attention from adopting any plan which might offer to effect their escape.

The heat soon became suffocating. We were parched with thirst, and there was not a drop of water in the house, and none to be procured nearer than the lake. I turned once more to the door, hoping that a passage might have been burnt through to the water. I saw nothing but a dense cloud of fire and smoke—could hear nothing but the crackling and roaring of flames, which were gaining so fast upon us that I felt their scorching breath in my face.

"Ah," thought I—and it was a most bitter thought—"what will my beloved husband say when he returns and finds that poor Susy and his dear girls have perished in this miserable manner? But God can save us yet."

The thought had scarcely found a voice in my heart before the wind rose to a hurricane, scattering the flames on all sides into a tempest of burning billows. I buried my head in my apron, for I thought that our time was come, and that all was lost, when a most terrific crash of thunder burst over our heads, and, like the breaking of a water-spout, down came the rushing torrent of rain which had been pent up for so many weeks. In a few minutes the chip-yard was all afloat, and the fire effectually checked. The storm which, unnoticed by us, had been gathering all day, and which was the only one of any note we had that summer, continued to rage all night, and before morning had quite subdued the cruel enemy, whose approach we had viewed with such dread.

The imminent danger in which we had been placed struck me more forcibly after it was past than at the time, and both the girl and myself sank upon our knees, and lifted up our hearts in humble thanksgiving to that God who had saved us by an act of His Providence from an awful and sudden death. When all hope from human assistance was lost, His hand was mercifully stretched forth, making His strength more perfectly manifested in our weakness:—

"He is their stay when earthly help is lost,
The light and anchor of the tempest-toss'd."

There was one person, unknown to us, who had watched the progress of that rash blaze, and had even brought his canoe to the landing, in the hope of getting us off. This was an Irish pensioner named Dunn, who had cleared a few acres on his government grant, and had built a shanty on the opposite shore of the lake.

"Faith, madam! an' I thought the captain was stark, staring mad to fire his fallow on such a windy day, and that blowing right from the lake to the house. When Old Wittals came in and towld us that the masther was not to the fore, but only one lad, an' the wife an' the chilther at home,—thinks I, there's no time to be lost, or the crathurs will be burnt up intirely. We started instanther, but, by Jove! we were too late. The swamp was all in a blaze when we got to the landing, and you might as well have tried to get to heaven by passing through the other place."

This was the eloquent harangue with which the honest creature informed me the next morning of the efforts he had made to save us, and the interest he had felt in our critical situation. I felt comforted for my past anxiety, by knowing that one human being, however humble, had sympathized in our probable fate; while the providential manner in which we had been rescued will ever remain a theme of wonder and gratitude.

The next evening brought the return of my husband, who listened to the tale of our escape with a pale and disturbed countenance; not a little thankful to find his wife and children still in the land of the living. For a long time after the burning of that fallow, it haunted me in my dreams. I would awake with a start, imagining myself fighting with the flames, and endeavouring to carry my little children through them to the top of the clearing, when invariably their garments and my own took fire just as I was within reach of a place of safety.

## CHAPTER IV.

### OUR LOGGING-BEE.

There was a man in our town,
In our town, in our town—
There was a man in our town,
He made a logging-bee;
And he bought lots of whiskey,
To make the loggers frisky—
To make the loggers frisky
At his logging-bee.

The Devil sat on a log heap,
A log heap, a log heap—
A red-hot burning log heap—
A-grinning at the bee;
And there was lots of swearing,
Of boasting and of daring,
Of fighting and of tearing,
At that logging-bee.

J. W. D. M.

A LOGGING-BEE followed the burning of the fallow, as a matter of course. In the bush, where hands are few, and labour commands an enormous rate of wages, these gatherings are considered indispensable, and much has been written in their praise; but, to me, they present the most disgusting picture of a bush life. They are noisy, riotous, drunken meetings, often terminating in violent quarrels, sometimes even in bloodshed. Accidents of the most serious nature often occur, and very little work is done, when we consider the number of hands employed, and the great consumption of food and liquor. I am certain, in our case, had we hired with the money expended in providing for the bee, two or three industrious, hard-working men, we should have got through twice as much work, and have had it done well, and have been the gainers in the end.

People in the woods have a craze for giving and going to bees, and run to them with as much eagerness as a peasant runs to a race-course or a fair; plenty of strong drink and excitement making the chief attraction of the bee. In raising a house or barn, a bee may be looked upon as a necessary evil, but these gatherings are generally conducted in a more orderly manner than those for logging. Fewer hands are required; and they are generally under the control of the carpenter who puts up the frame, and if they get drunk during the raising they are liable to meet with very serious accidents.

Thirty-two men, gentle and simple, were invited to our bee, and the maid and I were engaged for two days preceding the important one, in baking and cooking for the entertainment of our guests. When I looked at the quantity of food we had prepared, I thought that it never could be all eaten, even by thirty-two men. It was a burning-hot day towards the end of July, when our loggers began to come in, and the "gee!" and "ha!" of the oxen resounded on every side. There was my brother S——, with his frank English face, a host in himself; Lieutenant —— in his blouse, wide white trowsers, and red sash, his broad straw hat shading a dark manly face that would have been a splendid property for a bandit chief; the four gay, reckless, idle sons of ——, famous at any spree, but incapable of the least mental or physical exertion, who considered hunting and fishing as the sole aim and object of life. These young men rendered very little assistance themselves, and their example deterred others who were inclined to work.

There were the two R——s, who came to work and to make others work; my good brother-in-law, who had volunteered to be the Grog Bos, and a host of other settlers, among whom I recognized Moodie's old acquaintance, Dan Simpson, with his lank red hair and long freckled face: the Youngs, the hunters, with their round, black, curly heads and rich Irish brogue; poor C——, with his long, spare, consumptive figure, and thin, sickly face. Poor fellow, he has long since been gathered to his rest!

There was the ruffian quatter P——, from Clear Lake,—the dread of all honest men; the brutal M——, who treated oxen as if they had been logs, by beating them with handspikes; and there was Old Wittals, with his low forehead and long nose, a living witness of the truth of phrenology, if his large organ of acquisitiveness and his want of conscientiousness could be taken in evidence. Yet in spite of his derelictions from honesty, he was a hard-working, good-natured man, who, if he cheated you in a bargain, or took away some useful article in mistake from your homestead, never wronged his employer in his day's work.

He was a curious sample of cunning and simplicity—quite a character in his way—and the largest eater I ever chanced to know. From this ravenous propensity, for he eat his food like a famished wolf, he had obtained the singular name of "Wittals." During the first year of his settlement in the bush, with a very large family to provide for, he had been often in want of food. One day he came to my brother, with a very long face.

"'Fore God! Mr. S——, I'm no beggar, but I'd be obliged to you for a loaf of bread. I declare to you on my honour that I have not had a bit of wittals to dewour for two whole days."

He came to the right person with his petition. Mr. S——

with a liberal hand relieved his wants, but he entailed upon him the name of "Old Wittals," as part payment. His daughter, who was a very pretty girl, had stolen a march upon him into the wood, with a lad whom he by no means regarded with a favourable eye. When she returned, the old man confronted her and her lover with this threat, which I suppose he considered "the most awful" punishment that he could devise.

"March into the house, Madam 'Ria (Maria); and if ever I catch you with that scamp again, I'll tie you up to a stump all day, and give you no wittals."

I was greatly amused by overhearing a dialogue between Old Wittals and one of his youngest sons, a sharp, Yankeefied-looking boy, who had lost one of his eyes, but the remaining orb looked as if it could see all ways at once.

"I say, Sol, how came you to tell that tarnation tearing lie to Mr. S—— yesterday? Didn't you expect that you'd catch a good wallopping for the like of that? Lying may be excusable in a man, but 'tis a terrible bad habit in a boy."

"Lor', father, that worn't a lie. I told Mr. S——, our cow worn't in his peas. Nor more she wor: she was in his wheat."

"But she was in the peas all night, boy."

"That wor nothing to me; she worn't in just then. Sure I won't get a licking for that?"

"No, no, you are a good boy; but mind what I tell you, and don't bring me into a scrape with any of your real lies."

Prevarication, the worst of falsehoods, was a virtue in his eyes. So much for the old man's morality.

Monaghan was in his glory, prepared to work or fight, whichever should come uppermost; and there was old Thomas and his sons, the contractors for the clearing, to expedite whose movements the bee was called. Old Thomas was a very ambitious man in his way. Though he did not know A from B, he took it into his head that he had received a call from Heaven to convert the heathen in the wilderness; and every Sunday he held a meeting in our logger's shanty, for the purpose of awakening sinners, and bringing over "Injun pagans" to the true faith. His method of accomplishing this object was very ingenious. He got his wife, Peggy —or "my Paggy," as he called her—to read aloud for him a text from the Bible, until he knew it by heart; and he had, as he said truly, "a good remembrancer," and never heard a striking sermon but he retained the most important passages, and retailed them secondhand to his bush audience.

I must say that I was not a little surprised at the old man's eloquence when I went one Sunday over to the shanty to hear him preach. Several wild young fellows had come on purpose to make fun of him; but his discourse, which was upon the text, "We shall all meet before the judgment-seat of Christ," was rather too serious a subject to turn into a jest, with even old Thomas for the preacher. All went on very well until the old man gave out a hymn, and led off in such a loud, discordant voice, that my little Katie, who was standing between her father's knees, looked suddenly up, and said, "Mamma, what a noise old Thomas makes!" This remark led to a much greater noise, and the young men, unable to restrain their long-suppressed laughter, ran tumultuously from the shanty. I could have whipped the little elf; but small blame could be attached to a child of two years old, who had never heard a preacher, especially such a preacher as the old backwoodsman, in her life. Poor man! he was perfectly unconscious of the cause of the disturbance, and remarked to us, after the service was over,

"Well, ma'am, did not we get on famously? Now, worn't that a *bootiful* discourse?"

"It was, indeed; much better than I expected."

"Yes, yes; I knew it would please you. It had quite an effect on those wild fellows. A few more such sermons will teach them good behaviour. Ah! the bush is a bad place for young men. The farther in the bush, say I, the farther from God, and the nearer to hell. I told that wicked Captain I—— of Dummer so the other Sunday; 'an',' says he, 'if you don't hold your confounded jaw, you old fool, I'll kick you there.' Now, ma'am, now, sir, was not that bad manners in a gentleman, to use such *appropriate epitaphs* to a humble servant of God, like I?"

And thus the old man ran on for an hour, dilating upon his own merits and the sins of his neighbours.

There was John R——, from Smith-town, the most notorious swearer in the district; a man who esteemed himself clever, nor did he want for natural talent, but he had converted his mouth into such a sink of iniquity that it corrupted the whole man, and all the weak and thoughtless of his own sex who admitted him into their company. I had tried to convince John R—— (for he often frequented the house under the pretence of borrowing books) of the great crime that he was constantly committing, and of the injurious effect it must produce upon his own family, but the mental disease had taken too deep a root to be so easily cured. Like a person labouring under some foul disease, he contaminated all he touched. Such men seem to make an ambitious display of their bad habits in such scenes, and if they afford a little help, they are sure to get intoxicated and make a row. There was my friend, old Ned Dunn, who had been so anxious to get us out of the burning fallow. There was a whole group of Dummer Pines: Levi, the little wiry, witty poacher; Cornish Bill, the honest-hearted old peasant, with his stalwart figure and uncouth dialect; and David, and Ned—all good men and true; and Malachi Chroak, a queer, withered-up, monkey-man, that seemed like some mischievous elf, flitting from heap to heap to make work and fun for the rest; and many others were at that bee who have since found a rest in the wilderness: Adam T——, H——, J. M——, H. N——. These, at different times, lost their lives in those bright waters in which, on such occasions as these, they used to sport and frolic to refresh themselves during the noonday heat. Alas! how many, who were then young and in their prime, that river and its lakes have swept away!

Our men worked well until dinner-time, when, after washing in the lake, they all sat down to the rude board which I had prepared for them, loaded with the best fare that could be procured in the bush. Pea-soup, legs of pork, venison, eel, and raspberry pies, garnished with plenty of potatoes, and whiskey to wash them down, besides a large iron kettle of tea. To pour out the latter, and dispense it round, devolved upon me. My brother and his friends, who were all temperance men, and consequently the best workers in the field, kept me and the maid actively employed in replenishing their cups.

The dinner passed off tolerably well; some of the lower order of the Irish settlers were pretty far gone, but they committed no outrage upon our feelings by either swearing or bad language, a few harmless jokes alone circulating among them.

Some one was funning Old Wittals for having eaten seven large cabbages at Mr. T——'s bee, a few days previous. His son, Sol, thought himself, as in duty bound, to take up the cudgel for his father.

"Now, I guess that's a lie, anyhow. Faysther was sick that day, and I tell you he only ate five."

This announcement was followed by such an explosion of mirth that the boy looked fiercely round him, as if he could scarcely believe the fact that the whole party were laughing at him.

Malachi Chroak, who was good-naturedly drunk, had discovered an old pair of cracked bellows in a corner, which he placed under his arm, and applying his mouth to the pipe, and working his elbows to and fro, pretended that he was playing upon the bagpipes, every now and then letting the wind escape in a shrill squeak from this novel instrument.

"Arrah, ladies and jintlemen, do jist turn your swate little eyes upon me whilst I play for your iddifications the last illigant tune which my owld grandmother taught me. Och hone! 'tis a thousand pities that such musical owld crathurs should be suffered to die, at all at all, to be poked away into a dirthy, dark hole, when their canthles shud be burnin' a-top of a bushel, givin' light to the house. An' then it is she that was the illigant dancer, stepping out so lively and frisky, just so."

And here he minced to and fro, affecting the airs of a fine lady. The supposititious bagpipe gave an uncertain, ominous howl, and he flung it down, and started back with a ludicrous expression of alarm.

"Alive, is it ye are? Ye croaking owld divil, is that the tune you taught your son?

"Och! my owld granny taught me, but now she is dead,
That a dhrop of nate whiskey is good for the head;
It would make a man spake when jist ready to dhie,
If you doubt it—my boys!—I'd advise you to thry.

"Och! my owld granny sleeps with her head on a stone,—
'Now, Malach, don't throuble the gals when I'm gone!'
I thried to obey her; but, och, I am shure,
There's no sorrow on earth that the angels can't cure.

"Och! I took her advice—I'm a bachelor still;
And I dance, and I play, with such excellent skill,
(*Taking up the bellows, and beginning to dance.*)
That the dear little crathurs are striving in vain
Which first shall my hand or my fortin' obtain."

"Malach!" shouted a laughing group. "How was it that the old lady taught you to go a-courting?"

"Arrah, that's a sacret! I don't let out owld granny's sacrets," said Malachi, gracefully waving his head to and fro to the squeaking of the bellows; then, suddenly tossing back the long, dangling, black elf-locks that curled down the sides of his lank, yellow cheeks, and winking knowingly with his comical little deep-seated black eyes, he burst out again—

"Wid the blarney I'd win the most dainty proud dame,
No gal can resist the soft sound of that same;
Wid the blarney, my boys—if you doubt it, go thry—
But hand here the bottle, my whistle is dhry."

The men went back to the field, leaving Malachi to amuse those who remained in the house; and we certainly did laugh our fill at his odd capers and conceits.

Then he would insist upon marrying our maid. There could be no refusal—have her he would. The girl, to keep him quiet, laughingly promised that she would take him for her husband. This did not satisfy him. She must take her oath upon the Bible to that effect. Mary pretended that there was no bible in the house, but he found an old spelling-book upon a shelf in the kitchen, and upon it he made her swear, and called upon me to bear witness to her oath, that she was now his betrothed, and he would go next day with her to the "praist." Poor Mary had reason to repent her frolic, for he stuck close to her the whole evening, tormenting her to fulfil her contract. After the sun went down, the logging-band came in to supper, which was all ready for them. Those who remained sober ate the meal in peace, and quietly returned to their own homes; while the vicious and the drunken staid to brawl and fight.

After having placed the supper on the table, I was so tired

with the noise, and heat, and fatigue of the day, that I went to bed, leaving to Mary and my husband the care of the guests.

We were obliged to endure a second and a third repetition of this odious scene, before sixteen acres of land were rendered fit for the reception of our fall crop of wheat.

My hatred to these tumultuous, disorderly meetings was not in the least decreased by my husband being twice seriously hurt while attending them. After the second injury he received, he seldom went to them himself, but sent his oxen and servant in his place. In these odious gatherings, the sober, moral, and industrious man is more likely to suffer than the drunken and profane, as during the delirium of drink these men expose others to danger as well as themselves.

The conduct of many of the settlers, who considered themselves gentlemen, and would have been very much affronted to have been called otherwise, was often more reprehensible than that of the poor Irish emigrants, to whom they should have set an example of order and sobriety. The behaviour of these young men drew upon them the severe but just censures of the poorer class, whom they regarded in every way as their inferiors.

"That blackguard calls himself a gentleman. In what respect is he better than us?" was an observation too frequently made use of at these gatherings. To see a bad man in the very worst point of view, follow him to a bee; be he profane, licentious, quarrelsome, or a rogue, all his native wickedness will be fully developed there.

Just after the last of these logging-bees, we had to part with our good servant Mary, and just at a time when it was the heaviest loss to me. Her father, who had been a dairyman in the north of Ireland, an honest, industrious man, had brought out upwards of one hundred pounds to this country.

With more wisdom than is generally exercised by Irish emigrants, instead of sinking all his means in buying a bush farm, he hired a very good farm in Cavan, stocked it with cattle, and returned to his old avocation. The services of his daughter, who was an excellent dairymaid, were required to take the management of the cows; and her brother brought a wagon and horses all the way from the front to take her home.

This event was perfectly unexpected, and left me without a moment's notice to provide myself with another servant, at a time when servants were not to be had, and I was perfectly unable to do the least thing. My little Addie was sick almost to death with the summer complaint, and the eldest still too young to take care of herself.

This was but the beginning of trouble.

Ague and lake fever had attacked our new settlement. The men in the shanty were all down with it; and my husband was confined to his bed on each alternate day, unable to raise hand or foot, and raving in the delirium of the fever.

In my sister and brother's families, scarcely a healthy person remained to attend upon the sick; and at Herriot's Falls, nine persons were stretched upon the floor of one log cabin, unable to help themselves or one another. After much difficulty, and only by offering enormous wages, I succeeded in procuring a nurse to attend upon me during my confinement. The woman had not been a day in the house before she was attacked by the same fever. In the midst of this confusion, and with my precious little Addie lying insensible on a pillow at the foot of my bed—expected every moment to breathe her last sigh,—on the night of the 26th of August, the boy I had so ardently coveted was born. The next day, Old Pine carried his wife (my nurse) away upon his back, and I was left to struggle through, in the best manner I could, with a sick husband, a sick child, and a new-born babe.

It was a melancholy season, one of severe mental and bodily suffering. Those who have drawn such agreeable pictures of a residence in the backwoods never dwell upon the periods of sickness, when, far from medical advice, and often, as in my case, deprived of the assistance of friends by adverse circumstances, you are left to languish, unattended, upon the couch of pain. The day that my husband was free of the fit, he did what he could for me and his poor sick babes, but, ill as he was, he was obliged to sow the wheat to enable the man to proceed with the drag, and was therefore necessarily absent in the field the greater part of the day.

I was very ill, yet for hours at a time I had no friendly voice to cheer me, to proffer me a drink of cold water, or to attend to the poor babe; and worse, still worse, there was no one to help that pale, marble child, who lay so cold and still, with half-closed violet eye, as if death had already chilled her young heart in his iron grasp.

There was not a breath of air in our close, burning bed-closet; and the weather was sultry beyond all that I have since experienced. How I wished that I could be transported to an hospital at home, to enjoy the common care that in such places is bestowed upon the sick! Bitter tears flowed continually from my eyes over those young children. I had asked of Heaven a son, and there he lay helpless by the side of his almost equally helpless mother, who could not lift him up in her arms, or still his cries; while the pale, fair angel, with her golden curls, who had lately been the admiration of all who saw her, no longer recognized my voice, or was conscious of my presence. I felt that I could almost resign the long and eagerly hoped-for son, to win one more smile from that sweet, suffering creature. Often did I weep myself to sleep, and wake to weep again with renewed anguish.

And my poor little Katie, herself under three years of age,

how patiently she bore the loss of my care, and every comfort! How earnestly the dear thing strove to help me! She would sit on my sick-bed, and hold my hand, and ask me to look at her and speak to her; would inquire why Addie slept so long, and when she would awake again. Those innocent questions went like arrows to my heart. Lieutenant ———, the husband of my dear Emilia, at length heard of my situation. His inestimable wife was from home, nursing her sick mother; but he sent his maid-servant up every day for a couple of hours, and the kind girl despatched a messenger nine miles through the woods to Dummer, to fetch her younger sister, a child of twelve years old.

Oh, how grateful I felt for these signal mercies! for my situation for nearly a week was one of the most pitiable that could be imagined. The sickness was so prevalent that help was not to be obtained for money; and without the assistance of that little girl, young as she was, it is more than probable that neither myself nor my children would ever have risen from that bed of sickness.

The conduct of our man Jacob, during this trying period, was marked with the greatest kindness and consideration. On the days that his master was confined to his bed with the fever, he used to place a vessel of cold water and a cup by his bedside, and then put his honest English face in at my door to know if he could make a cup of tea, or toast a bit of bread for the mistress, before he went into the field.

Katie was indebted to him for all her meals. He baked, and cooked, and churned, milked the cows, and made up the butter, as well and as carefully as the best female servant could have done. As to poor John Monaghan, he was down with the fever in the shanty, where four other men were all ill with the same terrible complaint.

I was obliged to leave my bed and endeavour to attend to

the wants of my young family long before I was really able. When I made my first attempt to reach the parlour I was so weak, that, at every step, I felt as if I should pitch forward to the ground, which seemed to undulate beneath my feet like the floor of a cabin in a storm at sea. My husband continued to suffer for many weeks with the ague; and when he was convalescent, all the children, even the poor babe, were seized with it; nor did it leave us until late in the spring of 1835.

## CHAPTER V.

### A TRIP TO STONY LAKE.

MY husband had long promised me a trip to Stony Lake, and in the summer of 1835, before the harvest com menced, he gave Mr. Y——, who kept the mill at the rapids below Clear Lake, notice of our intention, and the worthy old man and his family made due preparation for our reception. The little girls were to accompany us.

We were to start at sunrise, to avoid the heat of the day, to go up as far as Mr. Y——'s in our canoe, re-embark with his sons above the rapids in birch-bark canoes, go as far up the lake as we could accomplish by daylight, and return at night; the weather being very warm, and the moon at full. Before six o'clock we were all seated in the little craft, which spread her white sail to a foaming breeze, and sped merrily over the blue waters. The lake on which our clearing stood was about a mile and a half in length, and about three quarters of a mile in breadth; a mere pond, when compared with the Bay of Quinté, Ontario, and the inland seas of Canada. But it was *our* lake, and, consequently, it had ten thousand beauties in our eyes, which would scarcely have attracted the observation of a stranger.

At the head of the Kutchawanook, the lake is divided by a long neck of land, that forms a small bay on the right-hand side, and a very brisk rapid on the left. The banks are formed of large masses of limestone; and the cardinal-flower and the tiger-lily seem to have taken an especial fancy to this spot, and to vie with each other in the display of their gorgeous colours.

It is an excellent place for fishing; the water is very deep close to the rocky pavement that forms the bank, and it has a pebbly bottom. Many a magic hour, at rosy dawn, or evening gray, have I spent with my husband on this romantic spot; our canoe fastened to a bush, and ourselves intent upon ensnaring the black bass, a fish of excellent flavour that abounds in this place.

Our paddles soon carried us past the narrows, and through the rapid water, the children sitting quietly at the bottom of the boat, enchanted with all they heard and saw, begging papa to stop and gather water-lilies, or to catch one of the splendid butterflies that hovered over us; and often the little Addie darted her white hand into the water to grasp at the shadow of the gorgeous insects as they skimmed along the waves.

After passing the rapids, the river widened into another small lake, perfectly round in form, and having in its centre a tiny green island, in the midst of which stood, like a shattered monument of bygone storms, one blasted, black ash-tree.

The Indians call this lake *Bessikákoon*, but I do not know the exact meaning of the word. Some say that it means "the Indian's grave;" others, "the lake of the one island." It is certain that an Indian girl is buried beneath that blighted tree; but I never could learn the particulars of her story, and perhaps there was no tale connected with it. She might have fallen a victim to disease during the wanderings of her tribe, and been buried on that spot; or she might have been drowned, which would account for her having been buried away from the rest of her people.

This little lake lies in the heart of the wilderness. There is but one clearing upon its shores, and that had been made by lumberers many years before; the place abounded with red cedar. A second growth of young timber had grown up in this spot, which was covered also with raspberry bushes—several hundred acres being entirely overgrown with this delicious berry.

It was here annually that we used to come in large picnic parties, to collect this valuable fruit for our winter preserves, in defiance of black-flies, mosquitoes, snakes, and even bears; all which have been encountered by berry-pickers upon this spot, as busy and as active as themselves, gathering an ample repast from Nature's bounteous lap.

And, oh! what beautiful wild shrubs and flowers grew up in that neglected spot! Some of the happiest hours I spent in the bush are connected with reminiscences of "Irving's shanty," for so the raspberry-grounds were called. The clearing could not be seen from the shore. You had to scramble through a cedar swamp to reach the sloping ground which produced the berries.

The mill at the Clear Lake rapids was about three miles distant from our own clearing; and after stemming another rapid, and passing between two beautiful wooded islands, the canoe rounded a point, and the rude structure was before us.

A wilder and more romantic spot than that which the old hunter had chosen for his homestead in the wilderness could scarcely be imagined. The waters of Clear Lake here empty themselves through a narrow, deep, rocky channel, not exceeding a quarter of a mile in length, and tumble over a limestone bridge of ten or twelve feet in height, which extends from one bank of the river to the other. The shores on either side are very steep, and the large oak-trees which have anchored their roots in every crevice of the rock, throw their fantastic arms far over the foaming waterfall, the deep green of their massy foliage forming a beautiful contrast with the white, flashing waters that foam over the shoot at least fifty feet below the brow of the limestone rock. By a flight of steps cut in the banks we ascended to the platform above the river on which Mr. Y——'s house stood.

It was a large, rough-looking, log building, surrounded by barns and sheds of the same primitive material. The porch before the door was covered with hops, and the room of general resort, into which it immediately opened, was of large dimensions, the huge fire-place forming the most striking feature. On the hearth-stone, hot as was the weather, blazed a great fire, encumbered with all sorts of culinary apparatus, which, I am inclined to think, had been called into requisition for our sole benefit and accommodation.

The good folks had breakfasted long before we started from home, but they would not hear of our proceeding to Stony Lake until after we had dined. It was only eight o'clock, A. M., and we had still four hours to dinner, which gave us ample leisure to listen to the old man's stories, ramble round the premises, and observe all the striking features of the place.

Mr. Y—— was a Catholic, and the son of a respectable farmer from the south of Ireland. Some few years before, he had emigrated with a large family of seven sons and two daughters, and being fond of field sports, and greatly taken with the beauty of the locality in which he had pitched his tent in the wilderness, he determined to raise a mill upon the dam which Nature had provided at his hands, and wait patiently until the increasing immigration should settle the township of Smith and Douro, render the property valuable, and bring plenty of grist to the mill. He was not far wrong in his calculations; and though, for the first few years, he subsisted entirely by hunting, fishing, and raising what potatoes and wheat he required for his own family, on the most fertile spots he could find on his barren lot, very little corn passed through the mill.

At the time we visited his place, he was driving a thriving trade, and all the wheat that was grown in the neighbourhood was brought by water to be ground at Y——'s mill. He had lost his wife a few years after coming to the country; but his two daughters, Betty and Norah, were excellent housewives, and amply supplied her loss. From these amiable women we received a most kind and hearty welcome, and every comfort and luxury within their reach. They appeared a most happy and contented family. The sons—a fine, hardy, independent set of fellows—were regarded by the old man with pride and affection. Many were his anecdotes of their prowess in hunting and fishing. His method of giving them an aversion to strong drink while very young amused me greatly, but it is not every child that could have stood the test of his experiment.

"When they were little chaps, from five to six years of age, I made them very drunk," he said; "so drunk that it brought on severe headache and sickness, and this so disgusted them with liquor, that they never could abide the sight of it again. I have only one drunkard among the seven; and he was such a weak, puling crathur, that I dared not play the same game with him, lest it should kill him. 'Tis his nature, I suppose, and he can't help it; but the truth is, that to make up for the sobriety of all the rest, he is killing himself with drink."

Norah gave us an account of her catching a deer that had got into the enclosure the day before.

"I went out," she said, "early in the morning, to milk the cows, and I saw a fine young buck struggling to get through a pale of the fence, in which having entangled his head and horns, I knew, by the desperate efforts he was making to push aside the rails, that if I was not quick in getting hold of him, he would soon be gone."

"And did you dare to touch him?"

"If I had had Mat's gun I would have shot him, but he would have made his escape long before I could run to the house for that, so I went boldly up to him and got him by the hind legs; and though he kicked and struggled dreadfully, I held on till Mat heard me call, and ran to my help, and cut his throat with his hunting-knife. So you see," she continued, with a good-natured laugh, "I can beat our hunters hollow—they hunt the deer, but I can catch a buck with my hands."

While we were chatting away, great were the preparations making by Miss Betty and a very handsome American woman, who had recently come thither as a help. One little barefooted garsoon was shelling peas in an Indian basket, another was stringing currants into a yellow pie-dish, and a third was sent to the rapids with his rod and line, to procure a dish of fresh fish to add to the long list of bush dainties that were preparing for our dinner. It was in vain that I begged our kind entertainers not to put themselves to the least trouble on our account, telling them that we were now used to the woods, and contented with any thing; they were determined to exhaust all their stores to furnish forth the entertainment. Nor can it be wondered at, that, with so many dishes to cook, and pies and custards to bake, instead of dining at twelve, it was past two o'clock before we were conducted to the dinner-table. I was vexed and disappointed at the delay, as I wanted to see all I could of the spot we were about to visit before night and darkness compelled us to return.

The feast was spread in a large outhouse, the table being formed of two broad deal boards laid together, and supported by rude carpenter's stools. A white linen cloth, a relic of better days, concealed these arrangements. The board was covered with an indescribable variety of roast and boiled, of fish, flesh, and fowl. My readers should see a table laid out in a wealthy Canadian farmer's house before they can have any idea of the profusion displayed in the entertainment of two visitors and their young children. Besides venison, pork, chickens, ducks, and fish of several kinds, cooked in a variety of ways, there was a number of pumpkin, raspberry, cherry, and currant pies, with fresh butter and green cheese (as the new cream-cheese is called), molasses, preserves, and pickled cucumbers, besides tea and coffee—the latter, be it known, I had watched the American woman boiling in the *frying-pan.* It was a black-looking compound, and I did not attempt to discuss its merits. The vessel in which it had been prepared had prejudiced me, and rendered me very skeptical on that score.

We were all very hungry, having tasted nothing since five o'clock in the morning, and contrived, out of the variety of good things before us, to make an excellent dinner.

I was glad, however, when we rose to prosecute our intended trip up the lake. The old man, whose heart was now thoroughly warmed with whiskey, declared that he meant to make one of the party, and Betty, too, was to accompany us; her sister Norah kindly staying behind to take care of the children. We followed a path along the top of the high ridge of limestone rock, until we had passed the falls and the rapids above, when we found Pat and Mat Y—— waiting for us on the shore below, in two beautiful new birch-bark canoes, which they had purchased the day before from the Indians.

Miss Betty, Mat, and myself, were safely stowed into one, while the old miller and his son Pat, and my husband, embarked in the other, and our steersmen pushed off into the middle of the deep and silent stream; the shadow of the tall woods, towering so many feet above us, casting an inky hue upon the waters. The scene was very imposing, and after paddling for a few minutes in shade and silence, we suddenly emerged into light and sunshine, and Clear Lake, which gets its name from the unrivalled brightness of its waters, spread out its azure mirror before us. The Indians regard this sheet of water with peculiar reverence. It abounds in the finest sorts of fish, the salmon-trout, the delicious white fish, muskenongé, and black and white bass. There is no island in this lake, no rice beds, nor stick nor stone, to break its tranquil beauty, and, at the time we visited it, there was but one clearing upon its shores.

The log hut of the squatter P——, commanding a beautiful prospect up and down the lake, stood upon a bold slope fronting the water; all the rest was unbroken forest. We had proceeded about a mile on our pleasant voyage, when our attention was attracted by a singular natural phenomenon, which Mat Y—— called the battery. On the right-hand side of the shore rose a steep, perpendicular wall of limestone, that had the appearance of having been laid by the hand of man, so smooth and even was its surface. After attaining a height of about fifty feet, a natural platform of eight or ten yards broke the perpendicular line of the rock, when another wall, like the first, rose to a considerable height, terminating in a second and third platform of the same description.

Fire, at some distant period, had run over these singularly beautiful terraces, and a second growth of poplars and balm-of-gileads relieved, by their tender green and light, airy foilage, the sombre indigo tint of the heavy pines that nodded like the plumes of a funeral-hearse over the fair young dwellers on the rock. The water is forty feet deep at the base of this precipice, which is washed by the waves. After we had passed the battery, Mat Y—— turned to me and said, "That is a famous place for bears; many a bear have I shot among those rocks."

This led to a long discussion on the wild beasts of the country.

"I do not think that there is much danger to be apprehended from them," said he; "but I once had an ugly adventure with a wolf two winters ago, on this lake."

I was all curiosity to hear the story, which sounded doubly interesting told on the very spot, and while gliding over those lovely waters.

"We were lumbering at the head of Stony Lake, about eight miles from here, my four brothers, myself, and several other hands. The winter was long and severe; although it was the first week in March, there was not the least appearance of a thaw, and the ice on these lakes was as firm as ever. I had been sent home to fetch a yoke of oxen to draw the saw-logs down to the water, our chopping being all completed, and the logs ready for rafting.

"I did not think it necessary to encumber myself with my rifle, and was, therefore, provided with no weapon of defence but the long gad I used to urge on the cattle. It was about four o'clock in the afternoon when I rounded Sandy Point, that long point which is about a mile ahead of us on the left shore, when I first discovered that I was followed, but at a great distance, by a large wolf. At first, I thought little of the circumstance, beyond a passing wish that I had brought my gun. I knew that he would not attack me before dark, and it was still two long hours to sundown; so I whistled, and urged on my oxen, and soon forgot the wolf—when, on stopping to repair a little damage to the peg of the yoke, I was surprised to find him close at my heels. I turned, and ran towards him, shouting as loud as I could, when he slunk back, but showed no inclination to make off. Knowing that he must have companions near, by his boldness, I shouted as loud as I could, hoping that my cries might be heard by my brothers, who would imagine that the oxen had got into the ice, and would come to my assistance. I was now winding my way through the islands in Stony Lake; the sun was setting red before me, and I had still three miles of my journey to accomplish. The wolf had become so impudent that I kept him off by pelting him with snowballs; and once he came so near that I struck him with the gad. I now began to be seriously alarmed, and from time to time shouted with all my strength; and you may imagine my joy when these cries were answered by the report of a gun. My brothers had heard me, and the discharge of a gun, for a moment, seemed to daunt the wolf. He uttered a long howl, which was answered by the cries of a large pack of the dirty brutes from the wood. It was only just light enough to distinguish objects, and I had to stop and face my enemy, to keep him at bay.

"I saw the skeleton forms of half-a-dozen more of them slinking among the bushes that skirted a low island; and tired and cold, I gave myself and the oxen up for lost, when I felt the ice tremble on which I stood, and heard men running at a distance. 'Fire your guns!' I cried out, as loud as I could. My order was obeyed, and such a yelling and howling immediately filled the whole forest as would have chilled your very heart. The thievish varmints instantly fled away into the bush.

"I never felt the least fear of wolves until that night; but when they meet in large bands, like cowardly dogs, they trust to their numbers, and grow fierce. If you meet with one wolf, you may be certain that the whole pack are at no great distance."

We were fast approaching Sandy Point, a long white ridge

of sand, running half across the lake, and though only covered with scattered groups of scrubby trees and brush, it effectually screened Stony Lake from our view. There were so many beautiful flowers peeping through the dwarf, green bushes, that, wishing to inspect them nearer, Mat kindly ran the canoe ashore, and told me that he would show me a pretty spot, where an Indian, who had been drowned during a storm off that point, was buried. I immediately recalled the story of Susan Moore's father, but Mat thought that he was interred upon one of the islands farther up.

"It is strange," he said, "that they are such bad swimmers. The Indian, though unrivalled by us whites in the use of the paddle, is an animal that does not take readily to the water, and those among them who can swim seldom use it as a recreation."

Pushing our way through the bushes, we came to a small opening in the underwood, so thickly grown over with wild Canadian roses in full blossom, that the air was impregnated with a delightful odour. In the centre of this bed of sweets rose the humble mound that protected the bones of the red man from the ravenous jaws of the wolf and the wild-cat. It was completely covered with stones, and from among the crevices had sprung a tuft of blue harebells, waving as wild and free as if they grew among the bonny red heather on the glorious hills of the North, or shook their tiny bells to the breeze on the broom-encircled commons of England.

The harebell had always from a child been with me a favourite flower; and the first sight of it in Canada, growing upon that lonely grave, so flooded my soul with remembrances of the past, that, in spite of myself, the tears poured freely from my eyes. There are moments when it is impossible to repress those outgushings of the heart—

"Those flood-gates of the soul that sever,
In passion's tide, to part for ever."

If Mat and his sister wondered at my tears, they must have suspected the cause, for they walked to a little distance, and left me to the indulgence of my feelings. I gathered those flowers, and placed them in my bosom, and kept them for many a day; they had become holy, when connected with sacred home recollections, and the never-dying affections of the heart which the sight of them recalled.

A shout from our companions in the other canoe made us retrace our steps to the shore. They had already rounded the point, and were wondering at our absence. Oh, what a magnificent scene of wild and lonely grandeur burst upon us as we swept round the little peninsula, and the whole majesty of Stony Lake broke upon us at once; another Lake of the Thousand Isles, in miniature, and in the heart of the wilderness! Imagine a large sheet of water, some fifteen miles in breadth and twenty-five in length, taken up by islands of every size and shape, from the lofty naked rock of red granite to the rounded hill, covered with oak-leaves to its summit; while others were level with the waters, and of a rich emerald green, only fringed with a growth of aquatic shrubs and flowers. Never did my eyes rest on a more lovely or beautiful scene. Not a vestige of man, or of his works, was there. The setting sun, that cast such a gorgeous flood of light upon this exquisite panorama, bringing out some of these lofty islands in strong relief, and casting others into intense shade, shed no cheery beam upon church spire or cottage pane. We beheld the landscape, savage and grand in its primeval beauty.

As we floated among the channels between these rocky picturesque isles, I asked Mat how many of them there were.

"I never could succeed," he said, "in counting them all.

One Sunday, Pat and I spent a whole day in going from one to the other, to try and make out how many there were, but we could only count up to one hundred and forty before we gave up the task in despair. There are a great many of them; more than any one would think—and, what is very singular, the channel between them is very deep, sometimes above forty feet, which accounts for the few rapids to be found in this lake. It is a glorious place for hunting; and the waters, undisturbed by steamboats, abound in all sorts of fish.

"Most of these islands are covered with huckleberries; while grapes, high and low-bush cranberries, blackberries, wild cherries, gooseberries, and several sorts of wild currants grow here in profusion. There is one island among these groups (but I never could light upon the identical one) where the Indians yearly gather their wampum-grass. They come here to collect the best birch-bark for their canoes, and to gather wild onions. In short, from the game, fish, and fruit, which they collect among the islands of this lake, they chiefly depend for their subsistence. They are very jealous of the settlers in the country coming to hunt and fish here, and tell many stories of wild beasts and rattlesnakes that abound along its shores; but I, who have frequented the lake for years, was never disturbed by any thing, beyond the adventure with the wolf, which I have already told you. The banks of this lake are all steep and rocky, and the land along the shore is barren, and totally unfit for cultivation.

"Had we time to run up a few miles further, I could have showed you some places well worth a journey to look at; but the sun is already down, and it will be dark before we get back to the mill."

The other canoe now floated alongside, and Pat agreed with his brother that it was high time to return. With reluctance I turned from this strangely fascinating scene. As we passed under one bold rocky island, Mat said, laughingly, "That is Mount Rascal."

"How did it obtain that name?"

"Oh, we were out here berrying, with our good priest, Mr. B——. This island promised so fair, that we landed upon it, and, after searching for an hour, we returned to the boat without a single berry, upon which Mr. B—— named it 'Mount Rascal.'"

The island was so beautiful, it did not deserve the name, and I christened it "Oak Hill," from the abundance of oak-trees which clothed its steep sides. The wood of this oak is so heavy and hard that it will not float in the water, and it is in great request for the runners of lumber-sleighs, which have to pass over very bad roads.

The breeze, which had rendered our sail up the lakes so expeditious and refreshing, had stiffened into a pretty high wind, which was dead against us all the way down. Betty now knelt in the bow and assisted her brother, squaw fashion, in paddling the canoe; but, in spite of all their united exertions, it was past ten o'clock before we reached the mill. The good Norah was waiting tea for us. She had given the children their supper four hours ago, and the little creatures, tired with using their feet all day, were sound asleep upon her bed.

After supper, several Irish songs were sung, while Pat played upon the fiddle, and Betty and Mat enlivened the company with an Irish jig.

It was midnight when the children were placed on my cloak at the bottom of the canoe, and we bade adieu to this hospitable family. The wind being dead against us, we were obliged to dispense with the sail, and take to our paddles. The moonlight was as bright as day, the air warm and balmy; and the aromatic, resinous smell exuded by the heat from the balm-of-gilead and the pine-trees in the forest, added greatly to our sense of enjoyment as we floated past scenes so wild and lonely—isles that assumed a mysterious look and character in that witching hour. In moments like these, I ceased to regret my separation from my native land; and, filled with the love of Nature, my heart forgot for the time the love of home. The very spirit of peace seemed to brood over the waters, which were broken into a thousand ripples of light by every breeze that stirred the rice blossoms, or whispered through the shivering aspen-trees. The far-off roar of the rapids, softened by distance, and the long, mournful cry of the night-owl, alone broke the silence of the night. Amid these lonely wilds the soul draws nearer to God, and is filled to overflowing by the overwhelming sense of His presence.

It was two o'clock in the morning when we fastened the canoe to the landing, and Moodie carried up the children to the house. I found the girl still up with my boy, who had been very restless during our absence. My heart reproached me, as I caught him to my breast, for leaving him so long; in a few minutes he was consoled for past sorrows, and sleeping sweetly in my arms.

## CHAPTER VI.

### DISAPPOINTED HOPES.

THE summer of '35 was very wet; a circumstance so unusual in Canada that I have seen no season like it during my sojourn in the country. Our wheat crop promised to be both excellent and abundant; and the clearing and seeding sixteen acres, one way or another, had cost us more than fifty pounds; still, we hoped to realize something handsome by the sale of the produce; and, as far as appearances went, all looked fair. The rain commenced about a week before the crop was fit for the sickle, and from that time until nearly the end of September was a mere succession of thunder showers; days of intense heat, succeeded by floods of rain. Our fine crop shared the fate of all other fine crops in the country; it was totally spoiled; the wheat grew in the sheaf, and we could scarcely save enough to supply us with bad, sticky bread; the rest was exchanged at the distillery for whiskey, which was the only produce which could be obtained for it. The store-keepers would not look at it, or give either money or goods for such a damaged article.

My husband and I had worked hard in the field; it was the first time I had ever tried my hand at field-labour, but our ready money was exhausted, and the steamboat stock had not paid us one farthing; we could not hire, and there was no help for it. I had a hard struggle with my pride before I would consent to render the least assistance on the farm, but reflection convinced me that I was wrong—that Providence had placed me in a situation where I was called upon to work—that it was not only my duty to obey that call, but to exert myself to the utmost to assist my husband, and help to maintain my family.

Ah, glorious poverty! thou art a hard taskmaster, but in thy soul-ennobling school, I have received more god-like lessons, have learned more sublime truths, than ever I acquired in the smooth highways of the world! The independent in soul can rise above the seeming disgrace of poverty, and hold fast their integrity, in defiance of the world and its selfish and unwise maxims. To them, no labour is too great, no trial too severe; they will unflinchingly exert every faculty of mind and body, before they will submit to become a burden to others.

The misfortunes that now crowded upon us were the result of no misconduct or extravagance on our part, but arose out of circumstances which we could not avert nor control. Finding too late the error into which we had fallen, in suffering ourselves to be cajoled and plundered out of our property by interested speculators, we braced our minds to bear the worst, and determined to meet our difficulties calmly and firmly, nor suffer our spirits to sink under calamities which energy and industry might eventually repair. Having once come to this resolution, we cheerfully shared together the labours of the field. One in heart and purpose, we dared remain true to ourselves, true to our high destiny as immortal creatures, in our conflict with temporal and physical wants. We found that manual toil, however distasteful to those unaccustomed to it, was not after all such a dreadful hardship; that the wilderness was not without its rose, the hard face of poverty without its smile. If we occasionally suffered severe pain, we as often experienced great pleasure, and I have contemplated a well-hoed ridge of potatoes on that bush farm, with as much delight as in years long past I had experienced in examining a fine painting in some well-appointed drawing-room.

I can now look back with calm thankfulness on that long period of trial and exertion—with thankfulness that the dark clouds that hung over us, threatening to blot us from existence, when they did burst upon us, were full of blessings. When our situation appeared perfectly desperate, then were we on the threshold of a new state of things, which was born out of that very distress.

In order more fully to illustrate the necessity of a perfect and childlike reliance upon the mercies of God—who, I most firmly believe, never deserts those who have placed their trust in Him—I will give a brief sketch of our lives during the years 1836 and 1837.

Still confidently expecting to realize an income, however small, from the steamboat stock, we had involved ourselves considerably in debt, in order to pay our servants and obtain the common necessaries of life; and we owed a large sum to two Englishmen in Dummer, for clearing ten more acres upon the farm. Our utter inability to meet these demands weighed very heavily upon my husband's mind. All superfluities in the way of groceries were now given up, and we were compelled to rest satisfied upon the produce of the farm. Milk, bread, and potatoes, during the summer became our chief, and often, for months, our only fare. As to tea and sugar, they were luxuries we would not think of, although I missed the tea very much; we rang the changes upon peppermint and sage, taking the one herb at our breakfast, the other at our tea, until I found an excellent substitute for both in the root of the dandelion.

The first year we came to this country, I met with an account of dandelion coffee, published in the *New York Albion*, given by a Dr. Harrison, of Edinburgh, who earnestly recommended it as an article of general use.

"It possesses," he says, "all the fine flavour and exhilarating properties of coffee, without any of its deleterious effects. The plant being of a soporific nature, the coffee made from it when drank at night produces a tendency to sleep, instead of exciting wakefulness, and may be safely used as a cheap and wholesome substitute for the Arabian berry, being equal in substance and flavour to the best Mocha coffee."

I was much struck with this paragraph at the time, and for several years felt a great inclination to try the Doctor's coffee; but something or other always came in the way, and it was put off till another opportunity. During the fall of '35, I was assisting my husband in taking up a crop of potatoes in the field, and observing a vast number of fine dandelion roots among the potatoes, it brought the dandelion coffee back to my memory, and I determined to try some for our supper. Without saying anything to my husband, I threw aside some of the roots, and when we left work, collecting a sufficient quantity for the experiment, I carefully washed the roots quite clean, without depriving them of the fine brown skin which covers them, and which contains the aromatic flavour, which so nearly resembles coffee that it is difficult to distinguish it from it while roasting. I cut my roots into small pieces, the size of a kidney-bean, and roasted them on an iron baking-pan in the stove-oven, until they were as brown and crisp as coffee. I then ground and transferred a small cupful of the powder to the coffee-pot, pouring upon it scalding water, and boiling it for a few minutes briskly over the fire. The result was beyond my expectations. The coffee proved excellent—far superior to the common coffee we procured at the stores.

To persons residing in the bush, and to whom tea and coffee are very expensive articles of luxury, the knowledge of this valuable property in a plant, scattered so abundantly through their fields, would prove highly beneficial. For years we used no other article; and my Indian friends who frequented the house gladly adopted the root, and made me show them the whole process of manufacturing it into coffee.

Experience taught me that the root of the dandelion is not so good, when applied to this purpose, in the spring as it is in the fall. I tried it in the spring, but the juice of the plant, having contributed to the production of leaves and flowers, was weak, and destitute of the fine bitter flavour so peculiar to coffee. The time of gathering in the potato crop is the best suited for collecting and drying the roots of the dandelion; and as they always abound in the same hills, both may be accomplished at the same time. Those who want to keep a quantity for winter use may wash and cut up the roots, and dry them on boards in the sun. They will keep for years, and can be roasted when required.

Few of our colonists are acquainted with the many uses to which this neglected but most valuable plant may be applied. I will point out a few which have come under my own observation, convinced as I am that the time will come when this hardy weed, with its golden flowers and curious seed-vessels, which form a constant plaything to the little children rolling about and luxuriating among the grass, in the sunny month of May, will be transplanted into our gardens, and tended with due care. The dandelion planted in trenches, and blanched to a beautiful cream-colour with straw, makes an excellent salad, quite equal to endive, and is more hardy and requires less care.

In many parts of the United States, particularly in new districts where vegetables are scarce, it is used early in the spring, and boiled with pork as a substitute for cabbage. During our residence in the bush we found it, in the early part of May, a great addition to the dinner-table. In the township of Dummer, the settlers boil the tops, and add hops to the liquor, which they ferment, and from which they obtain excellent beer. I have never tasted this simple beverage, but I have been told by those who use it that it is equal to the table-beer used at home.

Necessity has truly been termed the mother of invention, for I contrived to manufacture a variety of dishes almost out of nothing, while living in her school. When entirely destitute of animal food, the different variety of squirrels supplied us with pies, stews, and roasts. Our barn stood at the top of the hill near the bush, and in a trap set for such "small deer," we often caught from ten to twelve a-day.

The flesh of the black squirrel is equal to that of the rabbit, and the red, and even the little chissmunk, is palatable when nicely cooked. But from the lake, during the summer, we derived the larger portion of our food. The children called this piece of water "Mamma's pantry," and many a good meal has the munificent Father given to his poor dependent children from its well-stored depths. Moodie and I used to rise by daybreak, and fish for an hour after sunrise, when we returned, he to the field, and I to dress the little ones, clean up the house, assist with the milk, and prepare the breakfast.

Oh, how I enjoyed these excursions on the lake! The very idea of our dinner depending upon our success, added double zest to our sport.

One morning we started as usual before sunrise; a thick mist still hung like a fine veil upon the water when we pushed off, and anchored at our accustomed place. Just as the sun rose, and the haze parted and drew up like a golden sheet of transparent gauze, through which the dark woods loomed out like giants, a noble buck dashed into the water, followed by four Indian hounds.

We then discovered a canoe, full of Indians, just below the rapids, and another not many yards from us, that had been concealed by the fog. It was a noble sight, that gallant deer exerting all his energy, and stemming the water with such matchless grace, his branching horns held proudly aloft, his broad nostrils distended, and his fine eye fixed intently upon the opposite shore. Several rifle-balls whizzed past him, the dogs followed hard upon his track, but my very heart leaped for joy when, in spite of all his foes, his glossy hoofs spurned the opposite bank and he plunged headlong into the forest.

My beloved partner was most skilful in trolling for bass and muskinongé. His line he generally fastened to the paddle, and the motion of the oar gave a life-like vibration to the queer-looking mice and dragon-flies I used to manufacture from squirrel fur, or scarlet and white cloth, to tempt the finny wanderers of the wave.

When too busy himself to fish for our meals, little Katie and I ventured out alone in the canoe, which we anchored in any promising fishing spot, by fastening a harrow tooth to a piece of rope, and letting it drop from the side of the little vessel. By the time she was five years old, my little mermaid could both steer and paddle the light vessel, and catch small fish, which were useful for soup.

During the winter of '36, we experienced many privations. The ruffian squatter P——, from Clear Lake, drove from the barn a fine young bull we were rearing, and for several weeks all trace of the animal was lost. We had almost forgotten the existence of poor Whiskey, when a neighbour called and told Moodie that his yearling was at P——'s, and that he would advise him to get it back as soon as possible. Moodie had to take some wheat to Y——'s mill, and as the squatter lived only a mile further, he called at his house; and there, sure enough, he found the lost animal. With the greatest difficulty he succeeded in regaining his property, but not without many threats of vengeance from the parties who had stolen it. To these he paid no regard; but a few days after, six fat hogs, on which we depended for all our winter store of animal food, were driven into the lake, and destroyed. The death of these animals deprived us of three barrels of pork, and half starved us through the winter. That winter of '36, how heavily it wore away! The grown flour, frosted potatoes, and scant quantity of animal food rendered us all weak, and the children suffered much from the ague.

One day, just before the snow fell, Moodie had gone to Peterborough for letters; our servant was sick in bed with the ague, and I was nursing my little boy, Dunbar, who was shaking with the cold fit of his miserable fever, when Jacob put his honest, round, rosy face in at the door.

"Give me the master's gun, ma'am; there's a big buck feeding on the rice-bed near the island."

I took down the gun, saying, "Jacob, you have no chance; there is but one charge of buck-shot in the house."

"One chance is better nor none," said Jacob, as he commenced loading the gun. "Who knows what may happen to oie. Mayhap oie may chance to kill 'un; and you and the measter and the wee bairns may have zummut zavory for zupper yet."

Away walked Jacob with Moodie's "Manton" over his shoulder. A few minutes after, I heard the report of the gun, but never expected to see anything of the game; when Jacob suddenly bounced into the room, half wild with delight.

"Thae beast iz dead az a door-nail. Zure, how the measter will laugh when he zees the fine buck that oie a' zhot."

"And have you really shot him?"

"Come and zee! 'Tis worth your while to walk down to the landing to look at 'un."

Jacob got a rope, and I followed him to the landing, where, sure enough, lay a fine buck, fastened in tow of the canoe. Jacob soon secured him by the hind legs to the rope he had brought; and, with our united efforts, we at last succeeded in dragging our prize home. All the time he was engaged in taking off the skin, Jacob was anticipating the feast that we were to have; and the good fellow chuckled with delight when he hung the carcass quite close to the kitchen door, that his "measter" might run against it when he came home at night. This event actually took place. When Moodie opened the door, he struck his head against the dead deer.

"What have you got here?"

"A fine buck, zur," said Jacob, bringing forward the light, and holding it up in such a manner that all the merits of the prize could be seen at a glance.

"A fine one, indeed! How did we come by it?"

"It was zhot by oie," said Jacob, rubbing his hands in a sort of ecstacy. "Thae beast iz the first oie ever zhot in my life. He! he! he!"

"You shot that fine deer, Jacob?—and there was only one charge in the gun! Well done; you must have taken a good aim."

"Why, zur, oie took no aim at all. Oie just pointed the gun at the deer, and zhut my oeys an let fly at 'un. 'Twas Providence kill'd 'un, not oie."

"I believe you," said Moodie; "Providence has hitherto watched over us and kept us from actual starvation."

The flesh of the deer, and the good broth that I was able to obtain from it, greatly assisted in restoring our sick to health; but long before that severe winter terminated we were again out of food. Mrs. —— had given to Katie, in the fall, a very pretty little pig, which she had named Spot. The animal was a great favourite with Jacob and the children, and he always received his food from their hands at the door, and followed them all over the place like a dog. We had a noble hound called Hector, between whom and the pet pig there existed the most tender friendship. Spot always shared with Hector the hollow log which served him for a kennel, and we often laughed to see Hector lead Spot round the clearing by his ear. After bearing the want of animal food until our souls sickened at the bad potatoes and grown flour bread, we began—that is the eldest of the family—to cast very hungry eyes upon Spot; but no one liked to propose having him killed. At last Jacob spoke his mind upon the subject.

"Oi've heard, zur, that the Jews never eat pork; but we Christians dooz, and are right glad ov the chance. Now, zur, oi've been thinking that 'tis no manner ov use our keeping that beast Spot. If he wor a zow, now, there might be zome zenze in the thing; and we all feel weak for a morzel of meat. S'poze I kill him? He won't make a bad piece of pork."

Moodie seconded the move; and, in spite of the tears and prayers of Katie, her uncouth pet was sacrificed to the general wants of the family; but there were two members of the house who disdained to eat a morsel of the victim; poor Katie and the dog Hector. At the self-denial of the first I did not at all wonder, for she was a child full of sensibility and warm affections, but the attachment of the brute creature to his old playmate filled us all with surprise. Jacob first drew our attention to the strange fact.

"That dog," he said, as we were passing through the kitchen while he was at dinner, "do teach uz Christians a lesson how to treat our friends. Why, zur, he'll not eat a morzel of Spot. Oie have tried and tempted him in all manner ov ways, and he only do zneer and turn up his nose whei oie hould him a bit to taste." He offered the animal a ril of the fresh pork as he finished speaking, and the dog turned away with an expression of aversion, and on a repetition of the act, walked from the table. Human affection could scarcely have surpassed the love felt by this poor animal for his playfellow. His attachment to Spot, that could overcome the pangs of hunger—for, like the rest of us, he was half starved—must have been strong indeed.

Jacob's attachment to us, in its simplicity and fidelity, greatly resembled that of the dog; and sometimes, like the dog, he would push himself in where he was not wanted, and gratuitously give his advice, and make remarks which were not required.

Mr. K——, from Cork, was asking Moodie many questions about the partridges of the country; and, among other things, he wanted to know by what token you were able to discover their favourite haunts. Before Moodie could answer this last query a voice responded, through a large crack in the boarded wall which separated us from the kitchen, "They al ways bides where they's drum." This announcement was received with a burst of laughter that greatly disconcerted the natural philosopher in the kitchen.

On the 21st of May of this year, my second son, Donald, was born. The poor fellow came in hard times. The cows had not calved, and our bill of fare, now minus the deer and Spot, only consisted of bad potatoes and still worse bread. I was rendered so weak by want of proper nourishment that my dear husband, for my sake, overcame his aversion to borrowing, and procured a quarter of mutton from a friend. This, with kindly presents from neighbours—often as badly off as ourselves—a loin of a young bear, and a basket, containing a loaf of bread, some tea, some fresh butter, and oatmeal, went far to save my life.

Shortly after my recovery, Jacob—the faithful, good Jacob

—was obliged to leave us, for we could no longer afford to pay wages. What was owing to him had to be settled by sacrificing our best cow, and a great many valuable articles of clothing from my husband's wardrobe. Nothing is more distressing than being obliged to part with articles of dress which you know that you cannot replace. Almost all my clothes had been appropriated to the payment of wages, or to obtain garments for the children, excepting my wedding-dress, and the beautiful baby-linen which had been made by the hands of dear and affectionate friends for my first-born. These were now exchanged for coarse, warm flannels, to shield her from the cold. Moodie and Jacob had chopped eight acres during the winter, but these had to be burnt off and logged-up before we could put in a crop of wheat for the ensuing fall. Had we been able to retain this industrious, kindly English lad, this would have been soon accomplished; but his wages, at the rate of thirty pounds per annum, were now utterly beyond our means.

Jacob had formed an attachment to my pretty maid, Mary Pine, and before going to the Southern States, to join an uncle who resided in Louisville, an opulent tradesman, who had promised to teach him his business, Jacob thought it as well to declare himself. The declaration took place on a log of wood near the back door, and from my chamber window I could both hear and see the parties, without being myself observed. Mary was seated very demurely at one end of the log, twisting the strings of her checked apron, and the loving Jacob was busily whittling the other extremity of their rustic seat. There was a long silence. Mary stole a look at Jacob, and he heaved a tremendous sigh, something between a yawn and a groan. "Meary," he said, "I must go."

"I knew that afore," returned the girl.

"I had zummat to zay to you, Meary. Do you think you

will miss oie?" (looking very affectionately, and twitching nearer.)

"What put that into your head, Jacob?" This was said very demurely.

"Oie thowt, maybe, Meary, that your feelings might be zummat loike my own. I feel zore about the heart, Meary, and it's all com' of parting with you. Don't you feel queerish, too?"

"Can't say that I do, Jacob. I shall soon see you again," (pulling violently at her apron-string.)

"Meary, oi'm afeard you don't feel like oie."

"P'r'aps not—women can't feel like men. I'm sorry that you are going, Jacob, for you have been very kind and obliging, and I wish you well."

"Meary," cried Jacob, growing desperate at her coyness, and getting quite close up to her, "will you marry oie? Say yeez or noa."

This was coming close to the point. Mary drew farther from him, and turned her head away.

"Meary," said Jacob, seizing upon the hand that held the apron-string, "do you think you can better yoursel'? If not—why, oie'm your man. Now, do just turn about your head and answer oie."

The girl turned round, and gave him a quick, shy glance, then burst out into a simpering laugh.

"Meary, will you take oie?" (jogging her elbow.)

"I will," cried the girl, jumping up from the log, and running into the house.

"Well, that bargain's made," said the lover, rubbing his hands; "and now, oie'll go and bid measter and missus good-buoy."

The poor fellow's eyes were full of tears, for the children, who loved him very much, clung, crying, about his knees.

"God bless yees all," sobbed the kind-hearted creature. "Doan't forget Jacob, for he'll neaver forget you. Good-buoy!"

Then turning to Mary, he threw his arms round her neck, and bestowed upon her fair cheek the most audible kiss I ever heard.

"And doan't you forget me, Meary. In two years oie will be back to marry you; and maybe oie may come back a rich man."

Mary, who was an exceedingly pretty girl, shed some tears at the parting; but in a few days she was as gay as ever, and listening with great attention to the praises bestowed upon her beauty by an old bachelor, who was her senior by five-and-twenty years. But then he had a good farm, a saddle mare, and plenty of stock, and was reputed to have saved money. The saddle mare seemed to have great weight in old Ralph T——h's wooing; and I used laughingly to remind Mary of her absent lover, and beg her not to marry Ralph T——h's mare.

# CHAPTER VII.

## THE LITTLE STUMPY MAN.

BEFORE I dismiss for ever the troubles and sorrows of 1836, I would fain introduce to the notice of my readers some of the odd characters with whom we became acquainted during that period. The first that starts vividly to my recollection is the picture of a short, stumpy, thick-set man—a British sailor, too—who came to stay one night under our roof, and took quiet possession of his quarters for nine months, and whom we were obliged to tolerate from the simple fact that we could not get rid of him.

During the fall, Moodie had met this individual (whom I will call Mr. Malcolm) in the mail-coach, going up to Toronto. Amused with his eccentric and blunt manners, and finding him a shrewd, clever fellow in conversation, Moodie told him that if ever he came into his part of the world he should be glad to renew their acquaintance. And so they parted, with mutual good-will, as men often part who have travelled a long journey in good fellowship together, without thinking it probable they should ever meet again.

The sugar season had just commenced with the spring thaw; Jacob had tapped a few trees in order to obtain sap to make molasses for the children, when his plans were frustrated by the illness of my husband, who was again attacked with the ague. Towards the close of a wet, sloppy night, while Jacob was in the wood, chopping, and our servant gone to my sister, who was ill, to help to wash, as I was busy baking bread for tea, my attention was aroused by a violent knocking at the door, and the furious barking of our dog, Hector. I ran to open it, when I found Hector's teeth clenched in the trowsers of a little, dark, thick-set man, who said in a gruff voice,

"Call off your dog. What the devil do you keep such an infernal brute about the house for? Is it to bite people who come to see you?"

Hector was the best-behaved, best-tempered animal in the world; he might have been called a gentlemanly dog. So little was there of the unmannerly puppy in his behaviour, that I was perfectly astonished at his ungracious conduct. I caught him by the collar, and not without some difficulty, succeeded in dragging him off.

"Is Captain Moodie within?" said the stranger.

"He is, sir. But he is ill in bed—too ill to be seen."

"Tell him a friend," (he laid a strong stress upon the last word,) "a particular friend must speak to him."

I now turned my eyes to the face of the speaker with some curiosity. I had taken him for a mechanic, from his dirty, slovenly appearance; and his physiognomy was so unpleasant that I did not credit his assertion that he was a friend of my husband, for I was certain that no man who possessed such a forbidding aspect could be regarded by Moodie as a friend. I was about to deliver his message, but the moment I let go Hector's collar, the dog was at him again.

"Don't strike him with your stick," I cried, throwing my arms over the faithful creature. "He is a powerful animal, and if you provoke him, he will kill you."

I at last succeeded in coaxing Hector into the girl's room, where I shut him up, while the stranger came into the kitchen, and walked to the fire to dry his wet clothes.

I immediately went into the parlour, where Moodie was lying upon a bed near the stove, to deliver the stranger's message; but before I could say a word, he dashed in after me, and going up to the bed held out his broad, coarse hand, with, "How are you, Mr. Moodie. You see I have accepted your kind invitation sooner than either you or I expected. If you will give me house-room for the night I shall be obliged to you."

This was said in a low, mysterious voice; and Moodie, who was still struggling with the hot fit of his disorder, and whose senses were not a little confused, stared at him with a look of vague bewilderment. The countenance of the stranger grew dark.

"You cannot have forgotten me—my name is Malcolm."

"Yes, yes; I remember you now," said the invalid, holding out his burning, feverish hand. To my home, *such as it is*, you are welcome."

I stood by in wondering astonishment, looking from one to the other, as I had no recollection of ever hearing my husband mention the name of the stranger; but as he had invited him to share our hospitality, I did my best to make him welcome, though in what manner he was to be accommodated puzzled me not a little. I placed the arm-chair by the fire, and told him that I would prepare tea for him as soon as I could.

"It may be as well to tell you, Mrs. Moodie," said he sulkily, for he was evidently displeased by my husband's want of recognition on his first entrance, "that I have had no dinner."

I sighed to myself, for I well knew that our larder boasted of no dainties; and from the animal expression of our guest's face, I rightly judged that he was fond of good living.

By the time I had fried a rasher of salt pork, and made a

pot of dandelion coffee, the bread I had been preparing was baked; but grown flour will not make light bread, and it was unusually heavy. For the first time I felt heartily ashamed of our humble fare. I was sure that he for whom it was provided was not one to pass it over in benevolent silence. "He might be a gentleman," I thought, "but he does not look like one;" and a confused idea of who he was, and where Moodie had met with him, began to float through my mind. I did not like the appearance of the man, but I consoled myself that he was only to stay for one night, and I could give up my bed for that one night, and sleep on a bed on the floor by my sick husband. When I re-entered the parlour to cover the table, I found Moodie fallen asleep, and Mr. Malcolm reading. As I placed the tea-things on the table, he raised his head, and regarded me with a gloomy stare. He was a strange-looking creature; his features were tolerably regular, his complexion dark, with a good colour, his very broad and round head was covered with a perfect mass of close, black, curling hair, which, in growth, texture, and hue, resembled the wiry, curly hide of a water-dog. His eyes and mouth were both well-shaped, but gave, by their sinister expression, an odious and doubtful meaning to the whole of his physiognomy. The eyes were cold, insolent, and cruel, and as green as the eyes of a cat. The mouth bespoke a sullen, determined, and sneering disposition, as if it belonged to one brutally obstinate, one who could not by any gentle means be persuaded from his purpose. Such a man in a passion would have been a terrible wild beast; but the current of his feelings seemed to flow in a deep sluggish channel, rather than in a violent or impetuous one; and, like William Penn, when he reconnoitred his unwelcome visitors through the keyhole of the door, I looked at my strange guest, and liked him not. Perhaps my distant and constrained manner made him painfully aware of the fact, for I am certain that, from that first hour of our acquaintance, a deep-rooted antipathy existed between us, which time seemed rather to strengthen than diminish.

He ate of his meal sparingly, and with evident disgust; the only remarks which dropped from him were:

"You make bad bread in the bush. Strange, that you can't keep your potatoes from the frost! I should have thought that you could have had things more comfortable in the woods."

"We have been very unfortunate," I said, "since we came to the woods. I am sorry that you should be obliged to share the poverty of the land. It would have given me much pleasure could I have set before you a more comfortable meal."

"Oh, don't mention it. So that I get good pork and potatoes I shall be contented."

What did these words imply?—an extension of his visit? I hoped that I was mistaken; but before I could lose any time in conjecture my husband awoke. The fit had left him, and he rose and dressed himself, and was soon chatting cheerfully with his guest.

Mr. Malcolm now informed him that he was hiding from the sheriff of the N——— district's officers, and that it would be conferring upon him a great favour if he would allow him to remain at his house for a few weeks.

"To tell you the truth, Malcolm," said Moodie, "we are so badly off that we can scarcely find food for ourselves and the children. It is out of our power to make you comfortable, or to keep an additional hand, without he is willing to render some little help on the farm. If you can do this, I will endeavour to get a few necessaries on credit, to make your stay more agreeable."

To this proposition Malcolm readily assented, not only

because it released him from all sense of obligation, but because it gave him a privilege to grumble.

Finding that his stay might extend to an indefinite period, I got Jacob to construct a rude bedstead out of two large chests that had transported some of our goods across the Atlantic, and which he put up in a corner of the parlour. This I provided with a small hair-mattress, and furnished with what bedding I could spare.

For the first fortnight of his sojourn, our guest did nothing but lie upon that bed, and read, and smoke, and drink whiskey and water from morning until night. By degrees he let out part of his history; but there was a mystery about him which he took good care never to clear up. He was the son of an officer in the navy, who had not only attained a very high rank in the service, but, for his gallant conduct, had been made a Knight-Companion of the Bath.

He had himself served his time as a midshipman on board his father's flag-ship, but had left the navy and accepted a commission in the Buenos-Ayrean service during the political struggles in that province; he had commanded a sort of privateer under the government, to whom, by his own account, he had rendered many very signal services. Why he left South America and came to Canada he kept a profound secret. He had indulged in very vicious and dissipated courses since he came to the province, and by his own account had spent upwards of four thousand pounds, in a manner not over creditable to himself. Finding that his friends would answer his bills no longer, he took possession of a grant of land obtained through his father's interest, up in Hersey, a barren township on the shores of Stony Lake; and, after putting up his shanty, and expending all his remaining means, he found that he did not possess one acre out of the whole four hundred that would yield a crop of potatoes. He was now considerably in debt, and the lands, such as they were, had been seized, with all his effects, by the sheriff, and a warrant was out for his own apprehension, which he contrived to elude during his sojourn with us. Money he had none; and, beyond the dirty fearnought blue seaman's jacket which he wore, a pair of trowsers of the coarse cloth of the country, an old black vest that had seen better days, and two blue-checked shirts, clothes he had none. He shaved but once a week, never combed his hair, and never washed himself. A dirtier or more slovenly creature never before was dignified by the title of a gentleman. He was, however, a man of good education, of excellent abilities, and possessed a bitter, sarcastic knowledge of the world; but he was selfish and unprincipled in the highest degree.

His shrewd observations and great conversational powers had first attracted my husband's attention, and, as men seldom show their bad qualities on a journey, he thought him a blunt, good fellow, who had travelled a great deal, and could render himself a very agreeable companion by a graphic relation of his adventures. He could be all this, when he chose to relax from his sullen, morose mood; and, much as I disliked him, I have listened with interest for hours to his droll descriptions of South American life and manners.

Naturally indolent, and a constitutional grumbler, it was with the greatest difficulty that Moodie could get him to do any thing beyond bringing a few pails of water from the swamp for the use of the house, and he has often passed me carrying water up from the lake without offering to relieve me of the burden. Mary, the betrothed of Jacob, called him a perfect beast; but he, returning good for evil, considered *her* a very pretty girl, and paid her so many uncouth attentions that he roused the jealousy of honest Jake, who vowed that he would give him a good "looming" if he only dared to lay a finger upon his sweetheart. With Jacob to back her, Mary treated the "zea-bear," as Jacob termed him, with vast disdain, and was so saucy to him that, forgetting his admiration, he declared he would like to serve her as the Indians had done a scolding woman in South America. They attacked her house during the absence of her husband, cut out her tongue, and nailed it to the door, by way of knocker; and he thought that all women who could not keep a civil tongue in their head should be served in the same manner.

"And what should be done to men who swear and use ondacent language?" quoth Mary, indignantly. "Their tongues should be slit, and given to the dogs. Faugh! You are such a nasty fellow that I don't think Hector would eat your tongue."

"I'll kill that beast," muttered Malcolm, as he walked away.

I remonstrated with him on the impropriety of bandying words with our servants. "You see," I said, "the disrespect with which they treat you; and if they presume upon your familiarity, to speak to our guest in this contemptuous manner, they will soon extend the same conduct to us."

"But, Mrs. Moodie, you should reprove them."

"I cannot, sir, while you continue, by taking liberties with the girl, and swearing at the man, to provoke them to retaliation."

"Swearing! What harm is there in swearing? A sailor cannot live without oaths."

"But a gentleman might, Mr. Malcolm. I should be sorry to consider you in any other light."

"Ah, you are such a prude—so methodistical—you make no allowance for circumstances! Surely, in the woods we may dispense with the hypocritical, conventional forms of society, and speak and act as we please."

"So you seem to think; but you see the result."

"I have never been used to the society of ladies, and I cannot fashion my words to please them; and I won't, that's more!" he muttered to himself, as he strode off to Moodie in the field. I wished from my very heart that he was once more on the deck of his piratical South American craft.

One night he insisted on going out in the canoe to spear muskinongé with Moodie. The evening turned out very chill and foggy, and, before twelve, they returned, with only one fish, and half frozen with cold. Malcolm had got twinges of rheumatism, and he fussed, and sulked, and swore, and quarrelled with every body and every thing, until Moodie, who was highly amused by his petulance, advised him to go to his bed, and pray for the happy restoration of his temper.

"Temper!" he cried, "I don't believe there's a good-tempered person in the world. It's all hypocrisy! I never had a good temper! My mother was an ill-tempered woman, and ruled my father, who was a confoundedly severe, domineering man. I was born in an ill temper. I was an ill-tempered child; I grew up an ill-tempered man. I feel worse than ill tempered now, and when I die it will be in an illtemper."

"Well," quoth I, "Moodie has made you a tumbler of hot punch, which may help to drive out the cold and the ill temper, and cure the rheumatism."

"Ay; your husband's a good fellow, and worth two of you, Mrs. Moodie. He makes some allowance for the weakness of human nature, and can excuse even my ill temper."

I did not choose to bandy words with him, and the next day the unfortunate creature was shaking with the ague. A more intractable, outrageous, *im*-patient I never had the ill fortune to nurse. During the cold fit, he did nothing but swear at the cold, and wished himself roasting; and during the fever, he swore at the heat, and wished that he was sitting, in no other garment than his shirt, on the north side of an ice-berg. And when the fit at last left him, he got up, and ate such quantities of fat pork, and drank so much whiskey-punch, that you would have imagined he had just arrived from a long journey, and had not tasted food for a couple of days.

He would not believe that fishing in the cold night-air upon the water had made him ill, but raved that it was all my fault for having laid my baby down on his bed while it was shaking with the ague.

Yet, if there were the least tenderness mixed up in his iron nature, it was the affection he displayed for that young child. Dunbar was just twenty months old, with bright, dark eyes, dimpled cheeks, and soft, flowing, golden hair, which fell round his infant face in rich curls. The merry, confiding little creature formed such a contrast to his own surly, unyielding temper, that, perhaps, that very circumstance made the bond of union between them. When in the house, the little boy was seldom out of his arms, and whatever were Malcolm's faults, he had none in the eyes of the child, who used to cling around his neck, and kiss his rough, unshaven cheeks with the greatest fondness.

"If I could afford it, Moodie," he said one day to my husband, "I should like to marry. I want some one upon whom I could vent my affections." And wanting that some one in the form of woman, he contented himself with venting them upon the child.

As the spring advanced, and after Jacob left us, he seemed ashamed of sitting in the house doing nothing, and therefore undertook to make us a garden, or "to make garden," as the Canadians term preparing a few vegetables for the season. I procured the necessary seeds, and watched with no small surprise the industry with which our strange visitor commenced operations. He repaired the broken fence, dug the ground with the greatest care, and laid it out with a skill and neatness of which I had believed him perfectly incapable. In less than three weeks, the whole plot presented a very pleasing prospect, and he was really elated by his success.

"At any rate," said he, "we shall no longer be starved on bad flour and potatoes. We shall have peas, and beans, and beets, and carrots, and cabbage in abundance; besides the plot I have reserved for cucumbers and melons."

"Ah," thought I, "does he, indeed, mean to stay with us until the melons are ripe?" and my heart died within me, for he not only was a great additional expense, but he gave a great deal of additional trouble, and entirely robbed us of all privacy, as our very parlour was converted into a bedroom for his accommodation; besides that, a man of his singularly dirty habits made a very disagreeable inmate.

The only redeeming point in his character, in my eyes, was his love for Dunbar. I could not entirely hate a man who was so fondly attached to my child. To the two little girls he was very cross, and often chased them from him with blows. He had, too, an odious way of finding fault with every thing. I never could cook to please him; and he tried in the most malicious way to induce Moodie to join in his complaints. All his schemes to make strife between us, however, failed, and were generally visited upon himself. In no way did he ever seek to render me the least assistance. Shortly after Jacob left us, Mary Price was offered higher wages by a family at Peterborough, and for some time I was left with four little children, and without a servant. Moodie always milked the cows, because I never could overcome my fear of cattle; and though I had occasionally milked when there was no one else in the way, it was in fear and trembling.

Moodie had to go down to Peterborough; but before he

went, he begged Malcolm to bring me what water and wood I required, and to stand by the cattle while I milked the cows, and he would himself be home before night. He started at six in the morning, and I got the pail to go and milk. Malcolm was lying upon his bed, reading.

"Mr. Malcolm, will you be so kind as to go with me to the fields for a few minutes while I milk?"

"Yes!" (then, with a sulky frown,) "but I want to finish what I am reading."

"I will not detain you long."

"Oh, no! I suppose about an hour. You are a shocking bad milker."

"True; I never went near a cow until I came to this country; and I have never been able to overcome my fear of them."

"More shame for you! A farmer's wife, and afraid of a cow! Why, these little children would laugh at you."

I did not reply, nor would I ask him again. I walked slowly to the field, and my indignation made me forget my fear. I had just finished milking, and with a brimming pail was preparing to climb the fence and return to the house, when a very wild ox we had came running with headlong speed from the wood. All my fears were alive again in a moment. I snatched up the pail, and, instead of climbing the fence and getting to the house, I ran with all the speed I could command down the steep hill towards the lake shore, my feet caught in a root of the many stumps in the path, and I fell to the ground, my pail rolling many yards ahead of me. Every drop of my milk was spilt upon the grass. The ox passed on. I gathered myself up and returned home. Malcolm was very fond of new milk, and he came to meet me at the door.

"Hi! hi!—Where's the milk?"

"No milk for the poor children to-day," said I, showing him the inside of the pail, with a sorrowful shake of the head, for it was no small loss to them and me.

"How the devil's that? So you were afraid to milk the cows. Come away, and I will keep off the buggaboos."

"I did milk them—no thanks to your kindness, Mr. Malcolm—but—"

"But what?"

"The ox frightened me, and I fell and spilt all the milk."

"Whew! Now don't go and tell your husband that it was all my fault; if you had had a little patience, I would have come when you asked me, but I don't choose to be dictated to, and I won't be made a slave by you or any one else."

"Then why do you stay, sir, where you consider yourself so treated?" said I. "We are all obliged to work to obtain bread; we give you the best share—surely the return we ask for it is but small."

"You make me feel my obligations to you when you ask me to do any thing; if you left it to my better feelings we should get on better."

"Perhaps you are right. I will never ask you to do any thing for me in future."

"Oh, now, that's all mock humility. In spite of the tears in your eyes, you are as angry with me as ever; but don't go to make mischief between me and Moodie. If you'll say nothing about my refusing to go with you, I'll milk the cows for you myself to-night."

"And can you milk?" said I, with some curiosity.

"Milk! Yes; and if I were not so confoundedly low-spirited and —— lazy, I could do a thousand other things too. But now, don't say a word about it to Moodie."

I made no promise; but my respect for him was not increased by his cowardly fear of reproof from Moodie, who treated him with a kindness and consideration which he did not deserve. The afternoon turned out very wet, and I was sorry that I should be troubled with his company all day in the house. I was making a shirt for Moodie from some cotton that had been sent me from home, and he placed himself by the side of the stove, just opposite, and continued to regard me for a long time with his usual sullen stare. I really felt half afraid of him.

"Don't you think me mad?" said he. "I have a brother deranged; he got a stroke of the sun in India, and lost his senses in consequence; but sometimes I think it runs in the family."

What answer could I give to this speech, but mere evasive commonplace?

"You won't say what you really think," he continued; "I know you hate me, and that makes me dislike you. Now what would you say if I told you I had committed a murder, and that it was the recollection of that circumstance that made me at times so restless and unhappy?"

I looked up in his face, not knowing what to believe.

"'Tis fact," said he, nodding his head; and I hoped that he would not go mad, like his brother, and kill me.

"Come, I'll tell you all about it; I know the world would laugh at me for calling such an act *murder;* and yet I have been such a miserable man ever since, that I *feel* it was.

"There was a noted leader among the rebel Buenos-Ayreans, whom the government wanted much to get hold of. He was a fine, dashing, handsome fellow; I had often seen him, but we never came to close quarters. One night, I was lying wrapped up in my poncho at the bottom of my boat, which was rocking in the surf, waiting for two of my men, who were gone on shore. There came to the shore, this man and one of his people, and they stood so near the boat, which I suppose they thought empty, that I could distinctly hear their conversation. I suppose it was the devil who tempted me to put a bullet through that man's heart. He was an enemy to the flag under which I fought, but he was no enemy to me—I had no right to become his executioner; but still the desire to kill him, for the mere deviltry of the thing, came so strongly upon me that I no longer tried to resist it. I rose slowly upon my knees; the moon was shining very bright at the time, both he and his companion were too earnestly engaged to see me, and I deliberately shot him through the body. He fell with a heavy groan back into the water; but I caught the last look he threw up to the moonlight skies before his eyes glazed in death. Oh, that look!—so full of despair, of unutterable anguish; it haunts me yet—it will haunt me for ever. I would not have cared if I had killed him in strife—but in cold blood, and he so unsuspicious of his doom! Yes, it was murder; I know by this constant tugging at my heart that it was murder. What do you say to it?"

"I should think as you do, Mr. Malcolm. It is a terrible thing to take away the life of a fellow-creature without the least provocation."

"Ah! I knew you would blame me; but he was an enemy after all; I had a right to kill him; I was hired by the government under whom I served to kill him: and who shall condemn me?"

"No one more than your own heart."

"It is not the heart, but the brain, that must decide in questions of right and wrong," said he. "I acted from impulse, and shot the man; had I reasoned upon it for five minutes, that man would be living now. But what's done cannot be undone. Did I ever show you the work I wrote upon South America?"

"Are you an author," said I, incredulously.

"To be sure I am. Murray offered me £100 for my manuscript, but I would not take it. Shall I read to you some passages from it?"

I am sorry to say that his behaviour in the morning was uppermost in my thoughts, and I had no repugnance in refusing.

"No, don't trouble yourself. I have the dinner to cook, and the children to attend to, which will cause a constant interruption; you had better defer it to some other time."

"I shan't ask you to listen to me again," said he, with a look of offended vanity; but he went to his trunk, and brought out a large MS., written on foolscap, which he commenced reading to himself with an air of great self-importance, glancing from time to time at me, and smiling disdainfully. Oh, how glad I was when the door opened, and the return of Moodie broke up this painful *tête-à-tête*.

From the sublime to the ridiculous is but a step. The very next day, Mr. Malcolm made his appearance before me, wrapped in a great-coat belonging to my husband, which literally came down to his heels. At this strange apparition, I fell a-laughing.

"For God's sake, Mrs. Moodie, lend me a pair of inexpressibles. I have met with an accident in crossing the fence, and mine are torn to shreds—gone to the devil entirely."

"Well, don't swear. I'll see what can be done for you."

I brought him a new pair of fine, drab-coloured kerseymere trowsers that had never been worn. Although he was eloquent in his thanks, I had no idea that he meant to keep them for his sole individual use from that day thenceforth. But after all, what was the man to do? He had no trowsers, and no money, and he could not take to the woods. Certainly his loss was not our gain. It was the old proverb reversed

The season for putting in the potatoes had now arrived. Malcolm volunteered to cut the sets, which was easy work that could be done in the house, and over which he could lounge and smoke; but Moodie told him that he must take his share in the field, that I had already sets enough saved to plant half-an-acre, and would have more prepared by the time they were required. With many growls and shrugs, he felt obliged to comply; and he performed his part pretty well, the execrations bestowed upon the mosquitoes and black-flies forming a sort of safety-valve to let off the concentrated venom of his temper. When he came in to dinner, he held out his hands to me.

"Look at these hands."

"They are blistered with the hoe."

"Look at my face."

"You are terribly disfigured by the black-flies. But Moodie suffers just as much, and says nothing."

"Bah!—The only consolation one feels for such annoyances is to complain. Oh, the woods!—the cursed woods!—how I wish I were out of them." The day was very warm, but in the afternoon I was surprised by a visit from an old maiden lady, a friend of mine from C——. She had walked up with a Mr. Crowe, from Peterborough, a young, brisk-looking farmer, in breeches and top-boots, just out from the old country, who, naturally enough, thought he would like to roost among the woods.

He was a little, lively, good-natured manny, with a real Anglo-Saxon face,—rosy, high cheek-boned, with full lips, and a turned-up nose; and, like most little men, was a great talker, and very full of himself. He had belonged to the secondary class of farmers, and was very vulgar, both in person and manners. I had just prepared tea for my visitors, when Malcolm and Moodie returned from the field. There was no affectation about the former. He was manly in his person, and blunt even to rudeness, and I saw by the quizzical look which he cast upon the spruce little Crowe that he was quietly quizzing him from head to heel. A neighbour had sent me a present of maple molasses, and Mr. Crowe was so fearful of spilling some of the rich syrup upon his drab shorts that he spread a large pocket-handkerchief over his knees, and tucked another under his chin. I felt very much inclined to laugh, but restrained the inclination as well as I could—and if the little creature would have sat still, I could have quelled my rebellious propensity altogether; but up he would jump at every word I said to him, and make me a low, jerking bow, often with his mouth quite full, and the treacherous molasses running over his chin.

Malcolm sat directly opposite to me and my volatile next-door neighbour. He saw the intense difficulty I had to keep my gravity, and was determined to make me laugh out. So, coming slyly behind my chair, he whispered in my ear, with the gravity of a judge, "Mrs. Moodie, that must have been the very chap who first jumped Jim Crowe."

This appeal obliged me to run from the table. Moodie was astonished at my rudeness; and Malcolm, as he resumed his seat, made the matter worse by saying, "I wonder what is the matter with Mrs. Moodie; she is certainly very hysterical this afternoon."

The potatoes were planted, and the season of strawberries, green peas, and young potatoes come, but still Malcolm remained our constant guest. He had grown so indolent, and gave himself so many airs, that Moodie was heartily sick of his company, and gave him many gentle hints to change his quarters; but our guest was determined to take no hint. For some reason best known to himself, perhaps out of sheer contradiction, which formed one great element in his character, he seemed obstinately bent upon remaining where he was. Moodie was busy under-bushing for a full fallow. Malcolm spent much of his time in the garden, or lounging about the house. I had baked an eel-pie for dinner, which if prepared well is by no means an unsavoury dish. Malcolm had cleaned some green peas, and washed the first young potatoes we had drawn that season, with his own hands, and he was reckoning upon the feast he should have on the potatoes with childish glee. The dinner at length was put upon the table. The vegetables were remarkably fine, and the pie looked very nice.

Moodie helped Malcolm, as he always did, very largely, and the other covered his plate with a portion of peas and potatoes, when, lo and behold! my gentleman began making a very wry face at the pie.

"What an infernal dish!" he cried, pushing away his plate with an air of great disgust. "These eels taste as if they had been stewed in oil. Moodie, you should teach your wife to be a better cook."

The hot blood burnt upon Moodie's cheek. I saw indignation blazing in his eye.

"If you don't like what is prepared for you, sir, you may leave the table, and my house, if you please. I will put up with your ungentlemanly and ungrateful conduct to Mrs. Moodie no longer."

Out stalked the offending party. I thought, to be sure, we had got rid of him; and though he deserved what was said to him, I was sorry for him. Moodie took his dinner, quietly remarking, "I wonder he could find it in his heart to leave those fine peas and potatoes."

He then went back to his work in the bush, and I cleared away the dishes, and churned, for I wanted butter for tea.

About four o'clock, Mr. Malcolm entered the room. "Mrs.

Moodie," said he, in a more cheerful voice than usual, "where's the boss?"

"In the wood, under-bushing." I felt dreadfully afraid that there would be blows between them.

"I hope, Mr. Malcolm, that you are not going to him with any intention of a fresh quarrel."

"Don't you think I have been punished enough by losing my dinner?" said he, with a grin. "I don't think we shall murder one another." He shouldered his axe, and went whistling away.

After striving for a long while to stifle my foolish fears, I took the baby in my arms, and little Dunbar by the hand, and ran up to the bush where Moodie was at work.

At first I only saw my husband, but the strokes of an axe at a little distance soon guided my eyes to the spot where Malcolm was working away, as if for dear life. Moodie smiled, and looked at me significantly.

"How could the fellow stomach what I said to him? Either great necessity or great meanness must be the cause of his knocking under. I don't know whether most to pity or despise him."

"Put up with it, dearest, for this once. He is not happy, and must be greatly distressed."

Malcolm kept aloof, ever and anon casting a furtive glance towards us; at last little Dunbar ran to him, and held up his arms to be kissed. The strange man snatched him to his bosom, and covered him with caresses. It might be love to the child that had quelled his sullen spirit, or he might really have cherished an affection for us deeper than his ugly temper would allow him to show. At all events, he joined us at tea as if nothing had happened, and we might truly say that he had obtained a new lease of his long visit. But what could not be effected by words or hints of ours was brought about a few days after by the silly observation of a child. He asked Katie to give him a kiss, and he would give her some raspberries he had gathered in the bush.

"I don't want them. Go away; I don't like you, *you little stumpy man!*"

His rage knew no bounds. He pushed the child from him, and vowed that he would leave the house that moment—that she could not have thought of such an expression herself; she must have been taught it by us. This was an entire misconception on his part; but he would not be convinced that he was wrong. Off he went, and Moodie called after him, "Malcolm, as I am sending to Peterborough to-morrow, the man shall take in your trunk." He was too angry even to turn and bid us good-bye; but we had not seen the last of him yet. Two months after, we were taking tea with a neighbour, who lived a mile below us on the small lake. Who should walk in but Mr. Malcolm? He greeted us with great warmth for him, and when we rose to take leave, he rose and walked home by our side. "Surely the little stumpy man is not returning to his old quarters?" I am still a babe in the affairs of men. Human nature has more strange varieties than any one menagerie can contain, and Malcolm was one of the oddest of her odd species.

That night he slept in his old bed below the parlour window, and for three months afterwards he stuck to us like a beaver. He seemed to have grown more kindly, or we had got more used to his eccentricities, and let him have his own way; certainly he behaved himself much better. He neither scolded the children nor interfered with the maid, nor quarrelled with me. He had greatly discontinued his bad habit of swearing, and he talked of himself and his future prospects with more hope and self-respect. His father had promised to send him a fresh supply of money, and he proposed to buy of Moodie the clergy reserve, and that they should farm the two places on shares. This offer was received with great joy, as an unlooked-for means of paying our debts, and extricating ourselves from present and overwhelming difficulties, and we looked upon the little stumpy man in the light of a benefactor.

So matters continued until Christmas-eve, when our visitor proposed walking into Peterborough, in order to give the children a treat of raisins to make a Christmas pudding.

"We will be quite merry to-morrow," he said. "I hope we shall eat many Christmas dinners together, and continue good friends."

He started, after breakfast, with the promise of coming back at night; but night came, the Christmas passed away, months and years fled away, but we never saw the little stumpy man again!

He went away that day with a stranger in a wagon from Peterborough, and never afterwards was seen in that part of Canada. We afterwards learned that he went to Texas, and it is thought that he was killed at St. Antonio; but this is mere conjecture. Whether dead or living, I feel convinced that

"We ne'er shall look upon his like again."

# CHAPTER VIII.

## THE FIRE.

THE early part of the winter of 1837, a year never to be forgotten in the annals of Canadian history, was very severe. During the month of February, the thermometer often ranged from eighteen to twenty-seven degrees below zero. Speaking of the coldness of one particular day, a genuine Brother Jonathan remarked, with charming simplicity, that it was thirty degrees below zero that morning, and it would have been much colder if the thermometer had been longer.

The morning of the seventh was so intensely cold that every thing liquid froze in the house. The wood that had been drawn for the fire was green, and it ignited too slowly to satisfy the shivering impatience of women and children; I vented mine in audibly grumbling over the wretched fire, at which I in vain endeavoured to thaw frozen bread, and to dress crying children.

It so happened that an old friend, the maiden lady before alluded to, had been staying with us for a few days. She had left us for a visit to my sister, and as some relatives of hers were about to return to Britain by the way of New York, and had offered to convey letters to friends at home, I had been busy all the day before preparing a packet for England. It was my intention to walk to my sister's with this packet, directly the important affair of breakfast had been discussed, but the extreme cold of the morning had occasioned such delay that it was late before the breakfast-things were cleared away.

After dressing, I found the air so keen that I could not venture out without some risk to my nose, and my husband kindly volunteered to go in my stead. I had hired a young Irish girl the day before. Her friends were only just located in our vicinity, and she had never seen a stove until she came to our house. After Moodie left, I suffered the fire to die away in the Franklin stove in the parlour, and went into the kitchen to prepare bread for the oven.

The girl, who was a good-natured creature, had heard me complain bitterly of the cold, and the impossibility of getting the green wood to burn, and she thought that she would see if she could not make a good fire for me and the children, against my work was done. Without saying one word about her intention, she slipped out through a door that opened from the parlour into the garden, ran round to the wood-yard, filled her lap with cedar chips, and, not knowing the nature of the stove, filled it entirely with the light wood.

Before I had the least idea of my danger, I was aroused from the completion of my task by the crackling and roaring of a large fire, and a suffocating smell of burning soot. I looked up at the kitchen cooking-stove. All was right there. I knew I had left no fire in the parlour stove; but not being able to account for the smoke and smell of burning, I opened the door, and to my dismay found the stove red hot, from the front plate to the topmost pipe that let out the smoke through the roof.

My first impulse was to plunge a blanket, snatched from the servant's bed, which stood in the kitchen, into cold water. This I thrust into the stove, and upon it I threw water, until all was cool below. I then ran up to the loft, and by exhausting all the water in the house, even to that contained in the boilers upon the fire, contrived to cool down the pipes which passed through the loft. I then sent the girl out of doors to look at the roof, which, as a very deep fall of snow had taken place the day before, I hoped would be completely covered, and safe from all danger of fire.

She quickly returned, stamping and tearing her hair, and making a variety of uncouth outcries, from which I gathered that the roof was in flames.

This was terrible news, with my husband absent, no man in the house, and a mile and a quarter from any other habitation. I ran out to ascertain the extent of the misfortune, and found a large fire burning in the roof between the two stone pipes. The heat of the fires had melted off all the snow, and a spark from the burning pipe had already ignited the shingles. A ladder, which for several months had stood against the house, had been moved two days before to the barn, which was at the top of the hill, near the road; there was no reaching the fire through that source. I got out the dining-table, and tried to throw water upon the roof by standing on a chair placed upon it, but I only expended the little water that remained in the boiler, without reaching the fire. The girl still continued weeping and lamenting.

"You must go for help," I said. "Run as fast as you can to my sister's, and fetch your master."

"And lave you, ma'arm, and the childher alone wid the burnin' house?"

"Yes, yes! Don't stay one moment."

"I have no shoes, ma'arm, and the snow is so deep."

"Put on your master's boots; make haste, or we shall be lost before help comes."

The girl put on the boots and started, shrieking "Fire!" the whole way. This was utterly useless, and only impeded her progress by exhausting her strength. After she had vanished from the head of the clearing into the wood, and I was left quite alone, with the house burning over my head, I paused one moment to reflect what had best be done.

The house was built of cedar logs; in all probability it would be consumed before any help could arrive. There was a brisk breeze blowing up from the frozen lake, and the thermometer stood at eighteen degrees below zero. We were placed between the two extremes of heat and cold, and there was as much danger to be apprehended from the one as the other. In the bewilderment of the moment, the direful extent of the calamity never struck me: we wanted but this to put the finishing stroke to our misfortunes, to be thrown naked, houseless, and penniless, upon the world. "*What shall I save first?*" was the thought just then uppermost in my mind. Bedding and clothing appeared the most essentially necessary, and without another moment's pause, I set to work with a right good will to drag all that I could from my burning home.

While little Agnes, Dunbar, and baby Donald filled the air with their cries, Katie, as if fully conscious of the importance of exertion, assisted me in carrying out sheets and blankets, and dragging trunks and boxes some way up the hill, to be out of the way of the burning brands when the roof should fall in.

How many anxious looks I gave to the head of the clearing as the fire increased, and large pieces of burning pine began to fall through the boarded ceiling, about the lower rooms where we were at work. The children I had kept under a large dresser in the kitchen, but it now appeared absolutely necessary to remove them to a place of safety. To expose the young, tender things to the direful cold was almost as bad as leaving them to the mercy of the fire. At last I hit upon a plan to keep them from freezing. I emptied all the clothes out of a large, deep chest of drawers, and dragged the empty drawers up the hill; these I lined with blankets, and placed a child in each drawer, covering it well over with the bedding, giving to little Agnes the charge of the baby to hold between her knees, and keep well covered until help should arrive. Ah, how long it seemed coming!

The roof was now burning like a brush-heap, and, unconsciously, the child and I were working under a shelf, upon which were deposited several pounds of gunpowder which had been procured for blasting a well, as all our water had to be brought up-hill from the lake. This gunpowder was in a stone jar, secured by a paper stopper; the shelf upon which it stood was on fire, but it was utterly forgotten by me at the time; and even afterwards, when my husband was working on the burning loft over it.

I found that I should not be able to take many more trips for goods. As I passed out of the parlour for the last time, Katie looked up at her father's flute, which was suspended upon two brackets, and said,

"Oh, dear mamma! do save papa's flute; he will be so sorry to lose it."

God bless the dear child for the thought! the flute was saved; and, as I succeeded in dragging out a heavy chest of clothes, and looked up once more despairingly to the road, I saw a man running at full speed. It was my husband. Help was at hand, and my heart uttered a deep thanksgiving as another and another figure came upon the scene.

I had not felt the intense cold, although without cap, or bonnet, or shawl; with my hands bare and exposed to the bitter, biting air. The intense excitement, the anxiety to save all I could, had so totally diverted my thoughts from myself, that I had felt nothing of the danger to which I had been exposed; but now that help was near, my knees trembled under me, I felt giddy and faint, and dark shadows seemed dancing before my eyes.

The moment my husband and brother-in-law entered the house, the latter exclaimed,

"Moodie, the house is gone; save what you can of your winter stores and furniture."

Moodie thought differently. Prompt and energetic in danger, and possessing admirable presence of mind and coolness when others yield to agitation and despair, he sprang upon the burning loft and called for water. Alas, there was none!

"Snow, snow; hand me up pailfuls of snow!"

Oh! it was bitter work filling those pails with frozen snow; but Mr. T—— and I worked at it as fast as we were able.

The violence of the fire was greatly checked by covering the boards of the loft with this snow. More help had now arrived. Young B—— and S—— had brought the ladder down with them from the barn, and were already cutting away the burning roof, and flinging the flaming brands into the deep snow.

"Mrs. Moodie, have you any pickled meat?"

"We have just killed one of our cows, and salted it for winter stores."

"Well, then, fling the beef into the snow, and let us have the brine."

This was an admirable plan. Wherever the brine wetted the shingles, the fire turned from it, and concentrated into one spot.

But I had not time to watch the brave workers on the roof. I was fast yielding to the effects of over-excitement and fatigue, when my brother's team dashed down the clearing, bringing my excellent old friend, Miss B——, and the servant-girl.

My brother sprang out, carried me back into the house,

and wrapped me up in one of the large blankets scattered about. In a few minutes I was seated with the dear children in the sleigh, and on the way to a place of warmth and safety. Katie alone suffered from the intense cold. The dear little creature's feet were severely frozen, but were fortunately restored by her uncle discovering the fact before she approached the fire, and rubbing them well with snow. In the mean while, the friends we had left so actively employed at the house succeeded in getting the fire under before it had destroyed the walls. The only accident that occurred was to a poor dog, that Moodie had called Snarleyowe. He was struck by a burning brand thrown from the house, and crept under the barn and died.

Beyond the damage done to the building, the loss of our potatoes and two sacks of flour, we had escaped in a manner almost miraculous. This fact shows how much can be done by persons working in union, without bustle and confusion, or running in each other's way. Here were six men, who, without the aid of water, succeeded in saving a building, which, at first sight, almost all of them had deemed past hope. In after years, when entirely burnt out in a disastrous fire that consumed almost all we were worth in the world, some four hundred persons were present, with a fire-engine to second their endeavours, yet all was lost. Every person seemed in the way; and though the fire was discovered immediately after it took place, nothing was done beyond saving some of the furniture.

Our party was too large to be billetted upon one family. Mrs. T—— took compassion upon Moodie, myself, and the baby, while their uncle received the three children to his hospitable home.

It was some weeks before Moodie succeeded in repairing the roof, the intense cold preventing any one from working in such an exposed situation. The news of our fire travelled far and wide. I was reported to have done prodigies, and to have saved the greater part of our household goods before help arrived. Reduced to plain prose, these prodigies shrink into the simple, and by no means marvellous fact, that during the excitement I dragged out chests which, under ordinary circumstances, I could not have moved; and that I was unconscious both of the cold and the danger to which I was exposed while working under a burning roof, which, had it fallen, would have buried both the children and myself under its ruins. These circumstances appeared far more alarming, as all real danger does, after they were past. The fright and over-exertion gave my health a shock from which I did not recover for several months, and made me so fearful of fire, that from that hour it haunts me like a nightmare. Let the night be ever so serene, all stoves must be shut up, and the hot embers covered with ashes, before I dare retire to rest; and the sight of a burning edifice, so common a spectacle in large towns in this country, makes me really ill. This feeling was greatly increased after a second fire, when, for some torturing minutes, a lovely boy, since drowned, was supposed to have perished in the burning house.

Our present fire led to a new train of circumstances, for it was the means of introducing to Moodie a young Irish gentleman, who was staying at my brother's house. John E—— was one of the best and gentlest of human beings. His father, a captain in the army, had died while his family were quite young, and had left his widow with scarcely any means beyond the pension she received at her husband's death, to bring up and educate a family of five children. A handsome, showy woman, Mrs. E—— soon married again; and the poor lads were thrown upon the world. The eldest, who had been educated for the Church, first came to Canada in the hope of getting some professorship in the college, or of opening a classical school. He was a handsome, gentlemanly, well-educated young man, but constitutionally indolent—a natural defect which seemed common to all the males of the family, and which was sufficiently indicated by their soft, silky, fair hair and milky complexion. R—— had the good sense to perceive that Canada was not the country for him. He spent a week under our roof, and we were much pleased with his elegant tastes and pursuits; but my husband strongly advised him to try and get a situation as a tutor in some family at home. This he afterwards obtained. He became tutor and travelling companion to the young Lord M——; and has since got an excellent living.

John, who had followed his brother to Canada without the means of transporting himself back again, was forced to remain, and was working with Mr. S—— for his board. He proposed to Moodie working his farm upon shares; and as we were unable to hire a man, Moodie gladly closed with his offer; and, during the time he remained with us, we had every reason to be pleased with the arrangement. It was always a humiliating feeling to our proud minds, that hirelings should witness our dreadful struggles with poverty, and the strange shifts we were forced to make in order to obtain even food. But John E—— had known and experienced all that we had suffered, in his own person, and was willing to share our home with all its privations. Warm-hearted, sincere, and truly affectionate—a gentleman in word, thought, and deed—we found his society and cheerful help a great comfort. Our odd meals became a subject of merriment, and the peppermint and sage tea drank with a better flavour when we had one who sympathized in all our trials, and shared all our toils, to partake of it with us.

The whole family soon became attached to our young

friend; and after the work of the day was over, greatly we enjoyed an hour's fishing on the lake. John E—— said that we had no right to murmur, as long as we had health, a happy home, and plenty of fresh fish, milk, and potatoes. Early in May, we received an old Irishwoman into our service, who for four years proved a most faithful and industrious creature. And what with John E—— to assist my husband on the farm, and old Jenny to help me to nurse the children, and manage the house, our affairs, if they were no better in a pecuniary point of view, at least presented a more pleasing aspect at home. We were always cheerful, and sometimes contented and even happy.

How great was the contrast between the character of our new inmate and that of Mr. Malcolm! The sufferings of the past year had been greatly increased by the intolerable nuisance of his company, while many additional debts had been contracted in order to obtain luxuries for him which we never dreamed of purchasing for ourselves. Instead of increasing my domestic toils, John did all in his power to lessen them; and it always grieved him to see me iron a shirt, or wash the least article of clothing for him. "You have too much to do already; I cannot bear to give you the least additional work," he would say. And he generally expressed the greatest satisfaction at my method of managing the house, and preparing our simple fare. The little ones he treated with the most affectionate kindness, and gathered the whole flock about his knees the moment he came in to his meals.

On a wet day, when no work could be done abroad, Moodie took up his flute, or read aloud to us, while John and I sat down to work. The young emigrant, early cast upon the world and his own resources, was an excellent hand at the needle. He would make or mend a shirt with the greatest precision and neatness, and cut out and manufacture his canvas trowsers and loose summer-coats with as much adroitness as the most experienced tailor; darn his socks, and mend his boots and shoes, and often volunteered to assist me in knitting the coarse yarn of the country into socks for the children, while he made them moccasins from the dressed deer-skins that we obtained from the Indians. Scrupulously neat and clean in his person, the only thing which seemed to ruffle his calm temper was the dirty work of logging; he hated to come in from the field with his person and clothes begrimed with charcoal and smoke. Old Jenny used to laugh at him for not being able to eat his meals without first washing his hands and face.

"Och! my dear heart, yer too particular intirely; we've no time in the woods to be clane." She would say to him, in answer to his request for soap and a towel, "An' is it soap yer a wantin'? I tell yer that that same is not to the fore; bating the throuble of making, it's little soap that the misthress can get to wash the clothes for us and the childher, widout yer wastin' it in makin' yer purty skin as white as a leddy's. Do, darlint, go down to the lake and wash there; that basin is big enough, any how." And John would laugh, and go down to the lake to wash, in order to appease the wrath of the old woman. John had a great dislike to cats, and even regarded with an evil eye our old pet cat, Peppermint, who had taken a great fancy to share his bed and board.

"If I tolerate our own cat," he would say, "I will not put up with such a nuisance as your friend Emilia sends us in the shape of her ugly Tom. Why, where in the world do you think I found that beast sleeping last night?"

I expressed my ignorance.

"In our potato-pot. Now, you will agree with me that potatoes dressed with cat's hair is not a very nice dish. The next time I catch Master Tom in the potato-pot, I will kill him."

"John, you are not in earnest. Mrs. —— would never forgive any injury done to Tom, who is a great favourite."

"Let her keep him at home, then. Think of the brute coming a mile through the woods to steal from us all he can find, and then sleeping off the effects of his depredations in the potato-pot."

I could not help laughing, but I begged John by no means to annoy Emilia by hurting her cat.

The next day, while sitting in the parlour at work, I heard a dreadful squall, and rushed to the rescue. John was standing, with a flushed cheek, grasping a large stick in his hand, and Tom was lying dead at his feet.

"Oh, the poor cat!"

"Yes, I have killed him; but I am sorry for it now. What will Mrs. —— say?"

"She must not know it. I have told you the story of the pig that Jacob killed. You had better bury it with the pig."

John was really sorry for having yielded, in a fit of passion, to do so cruel a thing; yet a few days after he got into a fresh scrape with Mrs. ——'s animals.

The hens were laying, up at the barn. John was very fond of fresh eggs, but some strange dog came daily and sucked the eggs. John had vowed to kill the first dog he found in the act. Mr. —— had a very fine bull-dog, which he valued very highly; but with Emilia, Chowder was an especial favourite. Bitterly had she bemoaned the fate of Tom, and many were the inquiries she made of us as to his sudden disappearance.

One afternoon John ran into the room. "My dear Mrs. Moodie, what is Mrs. ——'s dog like?"

"A large bull-dog, brindled black and white."

"Then, by Jove, I've shot him!"

"John, John! you mean me to quarrel in earnest with my friend. How could you do it?"

"Why, how the deuce should I know her dog from another? I caught the big thief in the very act of devouring the eggs from under your sitting hen, and I shot him dead without another thought. But I will bury him, and she will never find it out a bit more than she did who killed the cat."

Some time after this, Emilia returned from a visit at P——. The first thing she told me was the loss of the dog. She was so vexed at it, she had had him advertised, offering a reward for his recovery. I, of course, was called upon to sympathize with her, which I did with a very bad grace. "I did not like the beast," I said; "he was cross and fierce, and I was afraid to go up to her house while he was there."

"Yes; but to lose him so. It is so provoking; and him such a valuable animal. I could not tell how deeply she felt the loss. She would give four dollars to find out who had stolen him."

How near she came to making the grand discovery the sequel will show.

Instead of burying him with the murdered pig and cat, John had scratched a shallow grave in the garden, and concealed the dead brute.

After tea, Emilia requested to look at the garden; and I, perfectly unconscious that it contained the remains of the murdered Chowder, led the way. Mrs. ——, whilst gathering a handful of fine green peas, suddenly stooped, and looking earnestly at the ground, called to me.

"Come here, Susanna, and tell me what has been buried here. It looks like the tail of a dog."

She might have added, "of my dog." Murder, it seems, will out. By some strange chance, the grave that covered the mortal remains of Chowder had been disturbed, and the black tail of the dog was sticking out.

"What can it be?" said I, with an air of perfect innocence. "Shall I call Jenny, and dig it up?"

"Oh, no, my dear; it has a shocking smell, but it does look very much like Chowder's tail."

"Impossible! How could it come among my peas?"

"True. Besides, I saw Chowder, with my own eyes yesterday, following a team; and George C—— hopes to recover him for me."

"Indeed! I am glad to hear it. How these mosquitoes sting. Shall we go back to the house?"

While we returned to the house, John, who had overheard the whole conversation, hastily disinterred the body of Chowder, and placed him in the same mysterious grave with Tom and the pig. Moodie and his friend finished logging-up the eight acres which the former had cleared the previous winter; besides putting in a crop of peas and potatoes, and an acre of Indian corn, reserving the fallow for fall wheat; while we had the promise of a splendid crop of hay off the sixteen acres that had been cleared in 1834. We were all in high spirits, and every thing promised fair, until a very trifling circumstance again occasioned us much anxiety and trouble, and was the cause of our losing most of our crop.

Moodie was asked to attend a bee, which was called to construct a corduroy bridge over a very bad piece of road. He and J. E—— were obliged to go that morning with wheat to the mill, but Moodie lent his yoke of oxen for the work.

The driver selected for them at the bee was the brutal M——y, a savage Irishman, noted for his ill-treatment of cattle, especially if the animals did not belong to him. He gave one of the oxen such a severe blow over the loins with a handspike that the creature came home perfectly disabled, just as we wanted his services in the hay-field and harvest.

Moodie had no money to purchase, or even to hire, a mate for the other ox; but he and John hoped that by careful attendance upon the injured animal he might be restored to health in a few days. They conveyed him to a deserted clearing, a short distance from the farm, where he would be safe from injury from the rest of the cattle; and early every morning we went in the canoe to carry poor Duke a warm mash, and to watch the progress of his recovery.

Ah, ye who revel in this world's wealth, how little can you realize the importance which we, in our poverty, attached to the life of this valuable animal! Yes, it even became the subject of prayer, for the bread for ourselves and our little ones depended greatly upon his recovery. We were doomed to disappointment. After nursing him with the greatest attention and care for some weeks, the animal grew daily worse, and suffered such intense agony, as he lay groaning upon the ground, unable to rise, that John shot him to put him out of pain.

Here, then, were we left without oxen to draw in our hay, or secure our other crops. A neighbour, who had an odd ox, kindly lent us the use of him, when he was not employed on his own farm; and John and Moodie gave their own work for the occasional loan of a yoke of oxen for a day. But with all these drawbacks, and in spite of the assistance of old Jenny and myself in the field, a great deal of the produce was damaged before it could be secured. The whole summer we had to labour under this disadvantage. Our neighbours were all too busy to give us any help, and their own teams were employed in saving their crops. Fortunately, the few acres of wheat we had to reap were close to the barn, and we carried the sheaves thither by hand; old Jenny proving an invaluable help, both in the harvest and hay field.

Still, with all these misfortunes, Providence watched over us in a signal manner. We were never left entirely without food. Like the widow's cruise of oil, our means, though small, were never suffered to cease entirely. We had been for some days without meat, when Moodie came running in for his gun. A great she-bear was in the wheat-field at the edge of the wood, very busily employed in helping to harvest the crop. There was but one bullet, and a charge or two of buck-shot, in the house; but Moodie started to the wood with the single bullet in his gun, followed by a little terrier dog that belonged to John E——. Old Jenny was busy at the wash-tub, but the moment she saw her master running up the clearing, and knew the cause, she left her work, and snatching up the carving-knife, ran after him, that in case the bear should have the best of the fight, she would be there to help "the masther." Finding her shoes incommode her, she flung them off, in order to run faster. A few minutes after, came the report of the gun, and I heard Moodie halloo to E——, who was cutting stakes for a fence in the wood. I hardly thought it possible that he could have killed the bear, but I ran to the door to listen. The children were all excitement, which the sight of the black monster, borne down the clearing upon two poles, increased to the wildest demonstrations of joy. Moodie and John were carrying the prize, and old Jenny, brandishing her carving-knife, followed in the rear.

The rest of the evening was spent in skinning and cutting up and salting the ugly creature, whose flesh filled a barrel with excellent meat, in flavour resembling beef, while the short grain and juicy nature of the flesh gave to it the tenderness of mutton. This was quite a Godsend, and lasted us until we were able to kill two large, fat hogs, in the fall.

A few nights after, Moodie and I encountered the mate of Mrs. Bruin, while returning from a visit to Emilia, in the very depth of the wood.

We had been invited to meet our friend's father and mother, who had come up on a short visit to the woods; and the evening passed away so pleasantly that it was near midnight before the little party of friends separated. The moon was down. The wood, through which we had to return, was very dark; the ground being low and swampy, and the trees thick and tall. There was, in particular, one very ugly spot, where a small creek crossed the road. This creek could only be passed by foot-passengers scrambling over a fallen tree, which, in a dark night, was not very easy to find. I begged a torch of Mr. M——; but no torch could be found. Emilia laughed at my fears; still, knowing what a coward I was in the bush of a night, she found up about an inch of candle, which was all that remained from the evening's entertainment. This she put into an old lantern.

"It will not last you long; but it will carry you over the creek."

This was something gained, and off we set. It was so dark in the bush, that our dim candle looked like a solitary red spark in the intense surrounding darkness, and scarcely served to show us the path. We went chatting along, talking over the news of the evening, Hector running on before us, when I saw a pair of eyes glare upon us from the edge of the swamp, with the green, bright light emitted by the eyes of a cat.

"Did you see those terrible eyes, Moodie?" and I clung, trembling, to his arm.

"What eyes?" said he, feigning ignorance. "It's too dark to see any thing. The light is nearly gone, and, if you don't quicken your pace, and cross the tree before it goes out, you will, perhaps, get your feet wet by falling into the creek."

"Good heavens! I saw them again; and do just look at the dog."

Hector stopped suddenly, and, stretching himself along the ground, his nose resting between his fore-paws, began to whine and tremble. Presently he ran back to us, and crept under our feet. The cracking of branches, and the heavy tread of some large animal, sounded close beside us.

Moodie turned the open lantern in the direction from whence the sounds came, and shouted as loud as he could, at the same time endeavouring to urge forward the fear-stricken dog, whose cowardice was only equalled by my own.

Just at that critical moment the wick of the candle flickered a moment in the socket, and expired. We were left, in perfect darkness, alone with the bear—for such we supposed the animal to be.

My heart beat audibly; a cold perspiration was streaming down my face, but I neither shrieked nor attempted to run. I don't know how Moodie got me over the creek. One of my feet slipped into the water, but, expecting, as I did every moment, to be devoured by master Bruin, that was a thing of no consequence. My husband was laughing at my fears, and every now and then he turned towards our companion, who continued following us at no great distance, and gave him an encouraging shout. Glad enough was I when I saw the gleam of the light from our little cabin window shine out among the trees; and, the moment I got within the clearing, I ran, without stopping until I was safely within the house. John was sitting up for us, nursing Donald. He listened with great interest to our adventure with the bear, and thought that Bruin was very good to let us escape without one affectionate hug.

"Perhaps it would have been otherwise had he known, Moodie, that you had not only killed his good lady, but were dining sumptuously off her carcass every day."

The bear was determined to have something in return for the loss of his wife. Several nights after this, our slumbers were disturbed, about midnight, by an awful yell, and old Jenny shook violently at our chamber door.

"Masther, masther, dear!—Get up wid you this moment, or the bear will desthroy the cattle intirely."

Half asleep, Moodie sprang from his bed, seized his gun, and ran out. I threw my large cloak round me, struck a light, and followed him to the door. The moment the latter was unclosed, some calves that we were rearing rushed into the kitchen, closely followed by the larger beasts, who came bellowing headlong down the hill, pursued by the bear.

It was a laughable scene, as shown by that paltry tallow-candle. Moodie, in his night-shirt, taking aim at something in the darkness, surrounded by the terrified animals; old Jenny, with a large knife in her hand, holding on to the white skirts of her master's garment, making outcry loud enough to frighten away all the wild beasts in the bush—herself almost in a state of nudity.

"Och, maisther, dear! don't timpt the ill-conditioned crathur wid charging too near; think of the wife and the childher. Let me come at the rampaging baste, an' I'll stick the knife into the heart of him."

Moodie fired. The bear retreated up the clearing, with a low growl. Moodie and Jenny pursued him some way, but it was too dark to discern any object at a distance. I, for my part, stood at the open door, laughing until the tears ran down my cheeks, at the glaring eyes of the oxen, their ears erect, and their tails carried gracefully on a level with their backs, as they stared at me and the light, in blank astonishment.

The noise of the gun had just roused John E—— from his slumbers. He was no less amused than myself, until he saw that a fine yearling heifer was bleeding, and found, upon examination, that the poor animal, having been in the claws of the bear, was dangerously, if not mortally hurt.

"I hope," he cried, "that the brute has not touched my foal!" I pointed to the black face of the filly peeping over the back of an elderly cow.

"You see, John, that Bruin preferred veal; there's your 'horsey,' as Dunbar calls her, safe, and laughing at you."

Moodie and Jenny now returned from the pursuit of the bear. E—— fastened all the cattle into the back yard, close to the house. By daylight he and Moodie had started in chase of Bruin, whom they tracked by his blood some way into the bush; but here he entirely escaped their search.

# CHAPTER IX.

## THE OUTBREAK.

THE long-protracted harvest was at length brought to a close. Moodie had procured another ox from Dummer, by giving a note at six months' date for the payment; and he and John E—— were in the middle of sowing their fall crop of wheat, when the latter received a letter from the old country, which conveyed to him intelligence of the death of his mother, and of a legacy of two hundred pounds. It was necessary for him to return to claim the property, and though we felt his loss severely, we could not, without great selfishness, urge him to stay. John had formed an attachment to a young lady in the country, who, like himself, possessed no property. Their engagement, which had existed several years, had been dropped, from its utter hopelessness, by mutual consent. Still the young people continued to love each other, and to look forward to better days, when their prospects might improve so far that E—— would be able to pur chase a bush farm, and raise a house, however lowly, to shelter his Mary. He, like our friend Malcolm, had taken a fancy to buy a part of our block of land, which he could culti vate in partnership with Moodie, without being obliged to hire, when the same barn, cattle, and implements would serve for both. Anxious to free himself from the thraldom of debts which pressed him sore, Moodie offered to part with two hundred acres at less than they cost us, and the bargain was to be considered as concluded directly the money was forthcoming.

It was a sorrowful day when our young friend left us; he had been a constant inmate in the house for nine months, and not one unpleasant word had ever passed between us. He had rendered our sojourn in the woods more tolerable by his society, and sweetened our bitter lot by his friendship and sympathy. We both regarded him as a brother, and parted with him with sincere regret. As to old Jenny, she lifted up her voice and wept, consigning him to the care and protection of all the saints in the Irish calendar. For several days after John left us, a deep gloom pervaded the house. Our daily toil was performed with less cheerfulness and alacrity; we missed him at the evening board, and at the evening fire; and the children asked each day, with increasing earnestness, when dear E—— would return.

Moodie continued sowing his fall wheat. The task was nearly completed, and the chill October days were fast verging upon winter, when towards the evening of one of them he contrived—I know not how—to crawl down from the field at the head of the hill, faint and pale, and in great pain. He had broken the small bone of his leg. In dragging, among the stumps, the heavy machine (which is made in the form of the letter V, and is supplied with large iron teeth) had hitched upon a stump, and being swung off again by the motion of the oxen, had come with great force against his leg. At first he was struck down, and for some time was unable to rise; but at length he contrived to unyoke the team, and crawled partly on his hands and knees down the clearing.

What a sad, melancholy evening that was! Fortune seemed never tired of playing us some ugly trick. The hope which had so long sustained me seemed about to desert me altogether; when I saw him on whom we all depended for subsistence, and whose kindly voice ever cheered us under the pressure of calamity, smitten down hopeless, all my courage and faith in the goodness of the Divine Father seemed to forsake me, and I wept long and bitterly.

The next morning I went in search of a messenger to send to Peterborough for the doctor; but though I found and sent the messenger, the doctor never came. Perhaps he did not like to incur the expense of a fatiguing journey with small chance of obtaining a sufficient remuneration.

Our dear sufferer contrived, with assistance, to bandage his leg; and after the first week of rest had expired, he amused himself with making a pair of crutches, and in manufacturing Indian paddles for the canoe, axe-handles, and yokes for the oxen. It was wonderful with what serenity he bore this unexpected affliction. Buried in the obscurity of those woods, we knew nothing, heard nothing of the political state of the country, and were little aware of the revolution which was about to work a great change for us and for Canada.

The weather continued remarkably mild. The first great snow, which for years had ordinarily fallen between the 10th and 15th of November, still kept off. November passed on, and as all our firewood had to be chopped by old Jenny during the lameness of my husband, I was truly grateful to God for the continued mildness of the weather. On the 4th of December—that great day of the outbreak—Moodie was determined to take advantage of the open state of the lake to carry a large grist up to Y——'s mill. I urged upon him the danger of a man attempting to manage a canoe in rapid water, who was unable to stand without crutches; but Moodie saw that the children would need bread, and he was anxious to make the experiment.

Finding that I could not induce him to give up the journey, I determined to go with him. Old Wittals, who happened to come down that morning, assisted in placing the bags of wheat in the little vessel, and helped to place Moodie at the stern. With a sad, foreboding spirit I assisted to push off from the shore. The air was raw and cold, but our sail was not without its pleasure. The lake was very full from the heavy rains, and the canoe bounded over the waters with a free, springy motion. A slight frost had hung every little bush and spray along the shores with sparkling crystals. The red pigeon-berries, shining through their coating of ice, looked like cornelian beads set in silver, and strung from bush to bush. We found the rapids at the entrance of Bessikakoon Lake very hard to stem, and were so often carried back by the force of the water, that, cold as the air was, the great exertion which Moodie had to make use of to obtain the desired object, brought the perspiration out in big drops upon his forehead. His long confinement to the house and low diet had rendered him very weak.

The old miller received us in the most hearty and hospitable manner; and complimented me upon my courage in venturing upon the water in such cold, rough weather. Norah was married, but the kind Betty provided us an excellent dinner, while we waited for the grist to be ground.

It was near four o'clock when we started on our return. If there had been danger in going up the stream, there was more in coming down. The wind had changed, the air was frosty, keen, and biting, and Moodie's paddle came up from every dip into the water, loaded with ice. For my part, I had only to sit still at the bottom of the canoe, as we floated rapidly down with wind and tide. At the landing we were met by old Jenny, who had a long story to tell us, of which we could make neither head nor tail—how some gentleman had called during our absence, and left a large paper, all about the Queen and the Yankees; that there was war between Canada and the States; that Toronto had been burnt, and the governor killed, and I know not what other strange and monstrous statements. After much fatigue, Moodie climbed the hill, and we were once more safe by our own fireside. Here we found the elucidation of Jenny's marvellous tales: a copy of the Queen's proclamation, calling upon all loyal gentlemen to join in putting down the unnatural rebellion.

A letter from my sister explained the nature of the outbreak, and the astonishment with which the news had been received by all the settlers in the bush. My brother and my sister's husband had already gone off to join some of the numerous bands of gentlemen who were collecting from all quarters to march to the aid of Toronto, which it was said was besieged by the rebel force. She advised me not to suffer Moodie to leave home in his present weak state; but the spirit of my husband was aroused, he instantly obeyed what he considered the imperative call of duty, and told me to prepare him a few necessaries, that he might be ready to start early in the morning. Little sleep visited our eyes that night. We talked over the strange news for hours; our coming separation, and the probability that if things were as bad as they appeared to be, we might never meet again. Our affairs were in such a desperate condition that Moodie anticipated that any change must be for the better; it was impossible for them to be worse. But the poor, anxious wife thought only of a parting which to her put a finishing stroke to all her misfortunes.

Before the cold, snowy morning broke, we were all stirring. The children, who had learned that their father was preparing to leave them, were crying and clinging round his knees. His heart was too deeply affected to eat; the meal passed over in silence, and he rose to go. I put on my hat and shawl to accompany him through the wood as far as my sister Mrs.

T——'s. The day was like our destiny, cold, dark, and lowering. I gave the dear invalid his crutches, and we commenced our sorrowful walk. Then old Jenny's lamentations burst forth, as, flinging her arms round my husband's neck, she kissed and blessed him after the fashion of her country.

"Och hone! och hone!" she cried, wringing her hands, "masther dear, why will you lave the wife and the childher? The poor crathur is breakin' her heart intirely at partin' wid you. Shure an' the war is nothin' to you, that you must be goin' into danger; an' you wid a broken leg. Och hone! och hone! come back to your home—you will be kilt, and thin what will become of the wife and the wee bairns?"

Her cries and lamentations followed us into the wood. At my sister's, Moodie and I parted; and with a heavy heart I retraced my steps through the wood. For once, I forgot all my fears. I never felt the cold. Sad tears were flowing over my cheeks; when I entered the house, hope seemed to have deserted me, and for upwards of an hour I lay upon the bed and wept. Poor Jenny did her best to comfort me, but all joy had vanished with him who was my light of life. Left in the most absolute uncertainty as to the real state of public affairs, I could only conjecture what might be the result of this sudden outbreak. Several poor settlers called at the house during the day, on their way down to Peterborough; but they brought with them the most exaggerated accounts. There had been a battle, they said, with the rebels, and the loyalists had been defeated; Toronto was besieged by sixty thousand men, and all the men in the backwoods were ordered to march instantly to the relief of the city.

In the evening, I received a note from Emilia, who was at Peterborough, in which she informed me that my husband had borrowed a horse of Mr. S——, and had joined a large party of two hundred volunteers, who had left that morning for Toronto; that there had been a battle with the insurgents; that Colonel Moodie had been killed, and the rebels had retreated; and that she hoped my husband would return in a few days. The honest backwoodsmen, perfectly ignorant of the abuses that had led to the present position of things, regarded the rebels as a set of monsters, for whom no punishment was too severe, and obeyed the call to arms with enthusiasm. The leader of the insurgents must have been astonished at the rapidity with which a large force was collected, as if by magic, to repel his designs. A great number of these volunteers were half-pay officers, many of whom had fought in the continental wars with the armies of Napoleon, and would have been found a host in themselves.

In a week, Moodie returned. So many volunteers had poured into Toronto that the number of friends was likely to prove as disastrous as that of enemies, on account of the want of supplies to maintain them all. The companies from the back townships had been remanded, and I received with delight my own again. But this reunion did not last long. Several regiments of militia were formed to defend the colony, and to my husband was given the rank of captain in one of those then stationed in Toronto.

On the 20th of January, 1838, he bade us a long adieu. I was left with old Jenny and the children to take care of the farm. It was a sad, dull time. I could bear up against all trials with him to comfort and cheer me, but his long-continued absence cast a gloom upon my spirit not easily to be shaken off. Still his very appointment to this situation was a signal act of mercy. From his full pay, he was enabled to liquidate many pressing debts, and to send home from time to time sums of money to procure necessaries for me and the little ones. These remittances were greatly wanted; but I demurred before laying them out for comforts which we had been so long used to dispense with. It seemed almost criminal to purchase any article of luxury, such as tea and sugar, while a debt remained unpaid.

The Y——'s were very pressing for the thirty pounds that we owed them for the clearing; but they had such a firm reliance upon the honour of my husband, that, poor and pressed for money as they were, they never sued us. I thought it would be a pleasing surprise to Moodie, if, with the sums of money which I occasionally received from him, I could diminish this debt, which had always given him the greatest uneasiness; and, my resolution once formed, I would not allow any temptation to shake it. The money was always transmitted to Dummer. I only reserved the sum of two dollars a-month, to pay a little lad to chop wood for us. After a time, I began to think the Y——'s were gifted with second-sight; for I never received a money-letter, but the very next day I was sure to see some of the family.

Just at this period I received a letter from a gentleman, requesting me to write for a magazine (the *Literary Garland*), just started in Montreal, with promise to remunerate me for my labours. Such an application was like a gleam of light springing up in the darkness; it seemed to promise the dawning of a brighter day. I had never been able to turn my thoughts towards literature during my sojourn in the bush. When the body is fatigued with labour, unwonted and beyond its strength, the mind is in no condition for mental occupation.

The year before, I had been requested by an American author, of great merit, to contribute to the *North American Review*, published for several years in Philadelphia; and he promised to remunerate me in proportion to the success of the work. I had contrived to write several articles after the children were asleep, though the expense even of the stationery and the postage of the manuscripts was severely felt by one so destitute of means; but the hope of being of the least service to those dear to me cheered me to the task. I never realized any thing from that source; but I believe it was not the fault of the editor. Several other American editors had written to me to furnish them with articles; but I was unable to pay the postage of heavy packets to the States, and they could not reach their destination without being paid to the frontier. Thus, all chance of making any thing in that way had been abandoned. I wrote to Mr. L——, and frankly informed him how I was situated. In the most liberal manner, he offered to pay the postage on all manuscripts to his office, and left me to name my own terms of remuneration. This opened up a new era in my existence; and for many years I have found in this generous man, to whom I am still personally unknown, a steady friend. I actually shed tears of joy over the first twenty-dollar bill I received from Montreal. It was my own; I had earned it with my own hand; and it seemed to my delighted fancy to form the nucleus out of which a future independence for my family might arise. I no longer retired to bed when the labours of the day were over. I sat up, and wrote by the light of a strange sort of candles, that Jenny called "sluts," and which the old woman manufactured out of pieces of old rags, twisted together and dipped in pork lard, and stuck in a bottle. They did not give a bad light, but it took a great many of them to last me for a few hours.

The faithful old creature regarded my writings with a jealous eye. "An', shure, it's killin' yerself that you are intirely. You were thin enough before you took to the pen; scribblin' an' scrabblin' when you should be in bed an' asleep. What good will it be to the childhren, dear heart! if you die afore your time, by wastin' your strength afther that fashion?"

Jenny never could conceive the use of books. "Shure,

we can live and die widout them. It's only a waste of time botherin' your brains wid the like of them; but, thank goodness! the lard will soon be all done, an' thin we shall hear you spakin' again, instead of sittin' there doubled up all night, desthroying your eyes wid porin' over the dirthy writin'."

As the sugar-making season drew near, Jenny conceived the bold thought of making a good *lump* of sugar, that the "childher" might have something to "ate" with their bread during the summer. We had no sugar-kettle, but a neighbour promised to lend us his, and to give us twenty-eight troughs, on condition that we gave him half the sugar we made. These terms were rather hard, but Jenny was so anxious to fulfil the darling object that we consented. Little Sol and the old woman made some fifty troughs more, the trees were duly tapped, a shanty in the bush was erected of small logs and brush and covered in at the top with straw; and the old woman and Solomon, the hired boy, commenced operations.

The very first day, a terrible accident happened to us; a large log fell upon the sugar-kettle—the borrowed sugar-kettle—and cracked it, spilling all the sap, and rendering the vessel, which had cost four dollars, useless. We were all in dismay. Just at that time Old Wittals happened to pass, on his way to Peterborough. He very good-naturedly offered to get the kettle repaired for us; which, he said, could be easily done by a rivet and an iron hoop. But where was the money to come from! I thought awhile. Katie had a magnificent coral and bells, the gift of her godfather; I asked the dear child if she would give it to buy another kettle for Mr. T——. She said, "I would give ten times as much to help mamma."

I wrote a little note to Emilia, who was still at her father's; and Mr. W——, the storekeeper, sent us a fine sugar-kettle back by Wittals, and also the other mended, in exchange for the useless piece of finery. We had now two kettles at work, to the joy of Jenny, who declared that it was a lucky fairy who had broken the old kettle.

While Jenny was engaged in boiling and gathering the sap in the bush, I sugared off the syrup in the house; an operation watched by the children with intense interest. After standing all day over the hot stove-fire, it was quite a refreshment to breathe the pure air at night. Every evening I ran up to see Jenny in the bush, singing and boiling down the sap in the front of her little shanty. The old woman was in her element, and afraid of nothing under the stars; she slept beside her kettles at night, and snapped her fingers at the idea of the least danger. She was sometimes rather despotic in her treatment of her attendant, Sol. One morning, in particular, she bestowed upon the lad a severe cuffing. I ran up the clearing to the rescue, when my ears were assailed by the "boo-hooing" of the boy.

"What has happened? Why do you beat the child, Jenny?"

"It's jist, thin, I that will bate him—the unlucky omadhawn! Has he not spilt and spiled two buckets of syrup, that I have been the live-long night bilin'. Sorra wid him; I'd like to strip the skin off him, I would! Musha! but 'tis enough to vex a saint."

"Ah, Jenny!" blubbered the poor boy, "but you have no mercy. You forget that I have but one eye, and that I could not see the root which caught my foot and threw me down."

"Faix! an' 'tis a pity that you have the one eye, when you don't know how to make a betther use of it," muttered the angry dame, as she picked up the pails, and, pushing him on before her, beat a retreat into the bush.

I was heartily sick of the sugar-making, long before the

season was over; however, we were well paid for our trouble. Besides one hundred and twelve pounds of fine soft sugar, as good as Muscovado, we had six gallons of molasses, and a keg containing six gallons of excellent vinegar.

Fifty pounds went to Mr. T——, for the use of his kettle; and the rest (with the exception of a cake for Emilia, which I had drained in a wet flannel bag until it was almost as white as loaf sugar) we kept for our own use. There was no lack, this year, of nice preserves and pickled cucumbers, dainties found in every native Canadian establishment.

Besides gaining a little money with my pen, I practised a method of painting birds and butterflies upon the white, velvety surface of the large fungi that grow plentifully upon the bark of the sugar-maple. These had an attractive appearance; and my brother, who was a captain in one of the provisional regiments, sold a great many of them among the officers, without saying by whom they were painted. One rich lady in Peterborough, long since dead, ordered two dozen to send as curiosities to England. These, at one shilling each, enabled me to buy shoes for the children, who, during our bad times, had been forced to dispense with these necessary coverings. How often, during the winter season, have I wept over their little chapped feet, literally washing them with my tears! But these days were to end; Providence was doing great things for us; and Hope raised at last her drooping head to regard with a brighter glance the far-off future.

Slowly the winter rolled away; but he to whom every thought turned was still distant from his humble home. The receipt of an occasional letter from him was my only solace during his long absence, and we were still too poor to indulge often in this luxury. My poor Katie was as anxious as her mother to hear from her father; and when I did get the long-looked-for prize, she would kneel down before me, her little elbows resting on my knees, her head thrown back, and the tears trickling down her innocent cheeks, eagerly drinking in every word.

The spring brought us plenty of work; we had potatoes and corn to plant, and the garden to cultivate. By lending my oxen for two days' work, I got Wittals, who had no oxen, to drag me in a few acres of oats, and to prepare the land for potatoes and corn. The former I dropped into the earth, while Jenny covered them up with the hoe.

Our garden was well dug and plentifully manured, the old woman bringing the manure, which had lain for several years at the barn door, down to the plot, in a large Indian basket placed upon a hand-sleigh. We had soon every sort of vegetable sown, with plenty of melons and cucumbers, and all our beds promised a good return. There were large flights of ducks upon the lake every night and morning; but though we had guns, we did not know how to use them. However, I thought of a plan, which I flattered myself might prove successful; I got Sol to plant two stakes in the shallow water, near the rice beds, and to these I attached a slender rope, made by braiding long strips of the inner bark of the basswood together; to these again I fastened, at regular intervals, about a quarter of a yard of whip-cord, headed by a strong perch-hook. These hooks I baited with fish offal, leaving them to float just under the water. Early next morning, I saw a fine black duck fluttering upon the line. The boy ran down with the paddles, but before he could reach the spot, the captive got away by carrying the hook and line with him. At the next stake he found upon the hooks a large eel and a catfish.

I had never before seen one of those whiskered, toad-like natives of the Canadian waters (so common to the Bay of Quinté, where they grow to a great size), that I was really terrified at the sight of the hideous beast, and told Sol to throw it away. In this I was very foolish, for they are esteemed good eating in many parts of Canada; but to me, the sight of the reptile-like thing is enough—it is uglier, and far more disgusting-looking than a toad.

When the trees came into leaf, and the meadows were green, and flushed with flowers, the poor children used to talk constantly to me of their father's return; their innocent prattle made me very sad. Every evening we walked into the wood, along the path that he must come whenever he did return home, to meet him; and though it was a vain hope, and the walk was taken just to amuse the little ones, I used to be silly enough to feel deeply disappointed when we returned alone. Donald, who was a mere baby when his father left us, could just begin to put words together. "Who is papa?" "When will he come?" "Will he come by the road?" "Will he come in a canoe?" The little creature's curiosity to see this unknown father was really amusing; and oh! how I longed to present the little fellow, with his rosy cheeks and curling hair, to his father; he was sc fair, so altogether charming in my eyes. Emilia had called him Cedric the Saxon; and he well suited the name, with his frank, honest disposition, and large, loving blue eyes.

June had commenced; the weather was very warm, and Mr. T—— had sent for the loan of old Jenny to help him for a day with his potatoes. I had just prepared dinner when the old woman came shrieking like a mad thing down the clearing, and waving her hands towards me. I could not imagine what had happened.

"Ninny's mad!" whispered Dunbar; "she's the old girl for making a noise."

"Joy! joy!" bawled out the old woman, now running

breathlessly towards us. "The masther's come—the masther's come!"

"Where?—where?"

"Jist above in the wood. Goodness gracious! I have run to let you know—so fast—that my heart—is like to—break."

Without stopping to comfort poor Jenny, off started the children and myself, at the very top of our speed; but I soon found that I could not run—I was too much agitated. I got to the head of the bush, and sat down upon a fallen tree. The children sprang forward like wild kids, all but Donald, who remained with his old nurse. I covered my face with my hands; my heart, too, was beating audibly; and now that he was come, and was so near me, I scarcely could command strength to meet him. The sound of happy young voices roused me up; the children were leading him along in triumph; and he was bending down to them, all smiles, but hot and tired with his long journey. It was almost worth our separation, that blissful meeting. In a few minutes he was at home, and the children upon his knees. Katie stood silently holding his hand, but Addie and Dunbar had a thousand things to tell him. Donald was frightened at his military dress, but he peeped at him from behind my gown, until I caught and placed him in his father's arms.

His leave of absence only extended to a fortnight. It had taken him three days to come all the way from Lake Erie, where his regiment was stationed, at Point Abino; and the same time would be consumed in his return. He could only remain with us eight days. How soon they fled away! How bitter was the thought of parting with him again! He had brought money to pay the J——'s. How surprised he was to find their large debt more than half liquidated. How gently did he chide me for depriving myself and the children of the little comforts he had designed for us, in order to make this sacrifice. But never was self-denial more fully rewarded; I felt happy in having contributed in the least to pay a just debt to kind and worthy people. You must become poor yourself before you can fully appreciate the good qualities of the poor—before you can sympathize with them, and fully recognize them as your brethren in the flesh. Their benevolence to each other, exercised amidst want and privation, as far surpasses the munificence of the rich towards them, as the exalted philanthropy of Christ and his disciples does the Christianity of the present day. The rich man gives from his abundance; the poor man shares with a distressed comrade his all.

One short, happy week too soon fled away, and we were once more alone. In the fall, my husband expected the regiment in which he held his commission would be reduced, which would again plunge us into the same distressing poverty. Often of a night I revolved these things in my mind, and perplexed myself with conjectures as to what in future was to become of us. Although he had saved all he could from his pay, it was impossible to pay several hundreds of pounds of debt; and the steamboat stock still continued a dead letter. To remain much longer in the woods was impossible, for the returns from the farm scarcely fed us; and but for the clothing sent us by friends from home, who were not aware of our real difficulties, we should have been badly off indeed.

I pondered over every plan that thought could devise; at last, I prayed to the Almighty to direct me as to what would be the best course for us to pursue. A sweet assurance stole over me, and soothed my spirit, that God would provide for us, as He had hitherto done—that a great deal of our distress arose from want of faith. I was just sinking into a calm sleep when the thought seemed whispered into my soul, "Write to the Governor; tell him candidly all you have suffered during your sojourn in this country; and trust to God for the rest."

At first I paid little heed to this suggestion; but it became so importunate that at last I determined to act upon it as if it were a message sent from heaven. I rose from my bed, struck a light, sat down, and wrote a letter to the Lieutenant-Governor, Sir George Arthur, a simple statement of facts, leaving it to his benevolence to pardon the liberty I had taken in addressing him.

I asked of him to continue my husband in the militia service, in the same regiment in which he now held the rank of captain, which, by enabling him to pay our debts, would rescue us from our present misery. Of the political character of Sir George Arthur I knew nothing. I addressed him as a man and a Christian; and I acknowledge, with the deepest and most heartfelt gratitude, the generous kindness of his conduct towards us. Before the day dawned, my letter was ready for the post. The first secret I ever had from my husband was the writing of that letter; and, proud and sensitive as he was, and averse to asking the least favour of the great, I was dreadfully afraid that the act I had just done would be displeasing to him; still, I felt resolutely determined to send it. After giving the children their breakfast, I walked down and read it to my brother-in-law, who was not only much pleased with its contents, but took it down himself to the post-office.

Shortly after, I received a letter from my husband, informing me that the regiment had been reduced, and that he should be home in time to get in the harvest. Most anxiously I awaited a reply to my application to the Governor; but no reply came.

The first week in August our dear Moodie came home, and brought with him, to our no small joy, J. E——, who had just returned from Ireland. E—— had been disappointed about the money, which was subject to litigation; and, tired of waiting at home until the tedious process of the law should terminate, he had come back to the woods, and, before night, was reinstated in his old quarters.

His presence made Jenny all alive; she dared him at once to a trial of skill with her in the wheat-field, which E—— prudently declined. He did not expect to stay longer in Canada than the fall, but, whilst he did stay, he was to consider our house his home.

That harvest was the happiest we ever spent in the bush. We had enough of the common necessaries of life. A spirit of peace and harmony pervaded our little dwelling, for the most affectionate attachment existed among its members. We were not troubled with servants, for the good old Jenny we regarded as an humble friend, and were freed, by that circumstance, from many of the cares and vexations of a bush life. Our evening excursions on the lake were doubly enjoyed after the labours of the day, and night brought us calm and healthful repose.

# CHAPTER X.

## THE WHIRLWIND.

THE 19th of August came, and our little harvest was all safely housed. Business called Moodie away for a few days to Cobourg. Jenny had gone to Dummer, to visit her friends, and J. E—— had taken a grist of the new wheat, which he and Moodie had threshed the day before, to the mill. I was consequently left alone with the children, and had a double portion of work to do. During their absence it was my lot to witness the most awful storm I ever beheld, and a vivid recollection of its terrors was permanently fixed upon my memory.

The weather had been intensely hot during the three preceding days, although the sun was entirely obscured by a blueish haze, which seemed to render the unusual heat of the atmosphere more oppressive. Not a breath of air stirred the vast forest, and the waters of the lake assumed a leaden hue. After passing a sleepless night, I arose, a little after daybreak, to superintend my domestic affairs. E—— took his breakfast, and went off to the mill, hoping that the rain would keep off until after his return.

"It is no joke," he said, "being upon these lakes in a small canoe, heavily laden, in a storm."

Before the sun rose, the heavens were covered with hard-looking clouds, of a deep blue and black cast, fading away to white at their edges, and in form resembling the long, rolling waves of a heavy sea—but with this difference, that the clouds were perfectly motionless, piled in long curved lines, one above the other, and so remained until four o'clock in the afternoon. The appearance of these clouds, as the sun rose above the horizon, was the most splendid that can be imagined, tinged up to the zenith with every shade of saffron, gold, rose-colour, scarlet, and crimson, fading away into the deepest violet. Never did the storm-fiend shake in the face of day a more gorgeous banner; and, pressed as I was for time, I stood gazing like one entranced upon the magnificent pageant.

As the day advanced, the same blue haze obscured the sun, which frowned redly through his misty veil. At ten o'clock the heat was suffocating, and I extinguished the fire in the cooking-stove, determined to make our meals upon bread and milk, rather than add to the oppressive heat. The thermometer in the shade ranged from ninety-six to ninety-eight degrees, and I gave over my work and retired with the little ones to the coolest part of the house. The young creatures stretched themselves upon the floor, unable to jump about or play; the dog lay panting in the shade; the fowls half buried themselves in the dust, with open beaks and outstretched wings. All nature seemed to droop beneath the scorching heat.

Unfortunately for me, a gentleman arrived about one o'clock from Kingston, to transact some business with my husband. He had not tasted food since six o'clock, and I was obliged to kindle the fire to prepare his dinner. It was one of the hardest tasks I ever performed; I almost fainted with the heat, and most inhospitably rejoiced when his dinner was over, and I saw him depart. Shortly afterwards, my friend Mrs. C—— and her brother called in, on their way from Peterborough.

"How do you bear the heat?" asked Mrs. C——. "This is one of the hottest days I ever remember to have experienced in this part of the province. I am afraid that it will end in a hurricane, or what the Lower Canadians term 'L'Orage.'"

About four o'clock they rose to go. I urged them to stay longer. "No," said Mrs. C——, "the sooner we get home the better. I think we can reach it before the storm breaks."

I took Donald in my arms, and my eldest boy by the hand, and walked with them to the brow of the hill, thinking that the air would be cooler in the shade. In this I was mistaken. The clouds over our heads hung so low, and the heat was so great, that I was soon glad to retrace my steps.

The moment I turned round to face the lake, I was surprised at the change that had taken place in the appearance of the heavens. The clouds, that had before lain so motionless, were now in rapid motion, hurrying and chasing each other round the horizon. It was a strangely awful sight. Before I felt a breath of the mighty blast that had already burst on the other side of the lake, branches of trees, leaves, and clouds of dust were whirled across the lake, whose waters rose in long sharp furrows, fringed with foam, as if moved in their depths by some unseen but powerful agent.

Panting with terror, I just reached the door of the house as the hurricane swept up the hill, crushing and overturning every thing in its course. Spell-bound, I stood at the open door, with clasped hands, unable to speak, rendered dumb and motionless by the terrible grandeur of the scene; while little Donald, who could not utter many intelligible words, crept to my feet, appealing to me for protection, while his rosy cheeks paled even to marble whiteness. The hurrying clouds gave to the heavens the appearance of a pointed dome, round which the lightning played in broad ribbons of fire. The roaring of the thunder, the rushing of the blast, the impetuous down-pouring of the rain, and the crash of falling trees, were perfectly deafening; and in the midst of this uproar of the elements, old Jenny burst in, drenched with wet, and half dead with fear.

"The Lord preserve us!" she cried, "this surely is the day of judgment. Fifty trees fell across my very path, between this an' the creek. Mrs. C—— just reached her brother's clearing a few minutes before a great oak fell on her very path. What thunther!—what lightning! Misthress, dear!—it's turn'd so dark, I can only jist see yer face."

Glad enough was I of her presence; for to be alone in the heart of the great forest, in a log hut, on such a night, was not a pleasing prospect. People gain courage by companionship, and in order to reassure each other, struggle to conceal their fears.

"And where is Mr. E——?"

"I hope not on the lake. He went early this morning to get the wheat ground at the mill."

"Och, the crathur! He's surely drowned. What boat could stan' such a scrimmage as this?"

I had my fears for poor John; but as the chance that he had to wait at the mill till others were served was more than probable, I tried to still my apprehensions for his safety. The storm soon passed over, after having levelled several acres of wood near the house, and smitten down in its progress two gigantic pines in the clearing, which must have withstood the force of a thousand winters. Talking over the effects of this whirlwind with my brother, he kindly sent me the following very graphic description of a whirlwind which passed through the town of Guelph in the summer of 1829.

* "In my hunting excursions and rambles through the Upper Canadian forests, I had frequently met with extensive wind-falls; and observed with some surprise that the fallen

* Written by Mr. Strickland, of Douro.

trees lay strewn in a succession of circles, and evidently appeared to have been twisted off the stumps. I also remarked that these wind-falls were generally narrow, and had the appearance of a road slashed through the forest. From observations made at the time, and since confirmed, I have no doubt that Colonel Reid's theory of storms is a correct one, viz., that all wind-storms move in a circular direction, and the nearer the centre the more violent the force of the wind. Having seen the effects of several similar hurricanes since my residence in Canada West, I shall proceed to describe one which happened in the township of Guelph during the early part of the summer of 1829.

"The weather, for the season of the year (May), had been hot and sultry, with scarcely a breath of wind stirring. I had heard distant thunder from an early hour in the morning, which, from the eastward, is rather an unusual occurrence. About 10 A. M., the sky had a most singular, and I must add a most awful appearance, presenting to the view a vast arch of rolling blackness, which seemed to gather strength and density as it approached the zenith. All at once the clouds began to work round in circles, as if chasing one another through the air. Suddenly the dark arch of clouds appeared to break up into detached masses, whirling and mixing through each other in dreadful commotion. The forked lightning was incessant, accompanied by heavy thunder. In a short time, the clouds seemed to converge to a point, which approached very near the earth, still whirling with great rapidity directly under this point; and apparently from the midst of the woods arose a black column, in the shape of a cone, which instantly joined itself to the depending cloud. The sight was now grand and awful in the extreme. Picture to your imagination a vast column of smoke, of inky blackness, reaching from earth to heaven, gyrating with fearful velocity—bright lightnings issuing from the vortex; the roar of the thunder—the rushing of the blast—the crash of timber—the limbs of trees, leaves, and rubbish, mingled with clouds of dust, whirling through the air;—you then have a faint idea of the scene.

"I had ample time for observation, as the hurricane commenced its devastating course about two miles from the town, through the centre of which it took its way, passing within fifty yards of where a number of persons, myself among the rest, were standing, watching its fearful progress.

"As the tornado approached, the trees seemed to fall like a pack of cards before its irresistible current. After passing through the clearing made around the village, the force of the wind gradually abated, and in a few minutes died away entirely.

"As soon as the storm was over, I went to see the damage it had done. From the point where I first observed the black column to rise from the woods and join the clouds, the trees were twisted in every direction. A belt of timber had been levelled to the ground, about two miles in length and about one hundred yards in breadth. At the entrance of the town it crossed the river Speed, and uprooted about six acres of wood, which had been thinned out, and left by Mr. Galt (late superintendent of the Canada Company), as an ornament to his house.

"The Eremosa road was completely blocked up for nearly half-a-mile, in the wildest confusion possible. In its progress through the town the storm unroofed several houses, levelled many fences to the ground, and entirely demolished a frame barn. Windows were dashed in; and, in one instance, the floor of a log house was carried through the roof. Some hair-breadth escapes occurred; but, luckily, no lives were lost.

"About twelve years since a similar storm occurred in the north part of the township of Douro, but was of much less magnitude. I heard an intelligent settler, who resided some years in the township of Madoc, state that, during his residence in that township, a similar hurricane to the one I have described, though of a much more awful character, passed through a part of Marmora and Madoc, and had been traced, in a north-easterly direction, upwards of forty miles into the unsurveyed lands; the uniform width of which appeared to be three quarters of a mile.

"It is very evident, from the traces which they have left behind them, that storms of this description have not been unfrequent in the wooded districts of Canada; and it becomes a matter of interesting consideration whether the clearing of our immense forests will not, in a great measure, remove the cause of these phenomena."

A few minutes after our household had retired to rest, my first sleep was broken by the voice of J. E——, speaking to old Jenny in the kitchen. He had been overtaken by the storm, but had run his canoe ashore upon an island before its full fury burst, and turned it over the flour; while he had to brave the terrors of a pitiless tempest—buffeted by the wind, and drenched with torrents of rain. I got up and made him a cup of tea, while Jenny prepared a rasher of bacon and eggs for his supper.

Shortly after this, J. E—— bade a final adieu to Canada, with his cousin C. W——. He volunteered into the Scotch Greys, and we never saw him more; but I have been told that he was so highly respected by the officers of the regiment that they subscribed for his commission; that he rose to the rank of lieutenant; accompanied the regiment to India, and was at the taking of Cabul; but from himself we never heard again.

The 16th of October, my third son was born; and a few days after, my husband was appointed paymaster to the militia regiments in the V. District, with the rank and full pay of captain.

This was Sir George Arthur's doing. He returned no answer to my application, but he did not forget us. As the time that Moodie might retain this situation was very doubtful, he thought it advisable not to remove me and the family until he could secure some permanent situation; by so doing, he would have a better opportunity of saving the greater part of his income to pay off his old debts.

This winter of 1839 was one of severe trial to me. Hitherto I had enjoyed the blessing of health; but both the children and myself were now doomed to suffer from dangerous attacks of illness. All the little things had malignant scarlet fever, and for several days I thought it would please the Almighty to take from me my two girls. This fever is so fatal to children in Canada that none of my neighbours dared approach the house. For three weeks Jenny and I were never undressed; our whole time was taken up in nursing the five little helpless creatures through the successive stages of their alarming disease. I sent for Dr. Taylor; but he did not come, and I was obliged to trust to the mercy of God, and my own judgment and good nursing. Though I escaped the fever, mental anxiety and fatigue brought on other illness, which for nearly ten weeks rendered me perfectly helpless. When I was again able to creep from my sick bed, the baby was seized with an illness, which Dr. B—— pronounced mortal. Against all hope, he recovered, but these severe mental trials rendered me weak and nervous, and more anxious than ever to be re-united to my husband. To add to these troubles, my sister and her husband sold their farm, and removed from our neighbourhood. Mr. —— had returned to England, and had obtained a situation in the Customs; and his wife, my friend Emilia, was keeping a school in the village; so that I felt more solitary than ever, thus deprived of so many kind, sympathizing friends.

# CHAPTER XI.

## THE WALK TO DUMMER.

READER! have you ever heard of a place situated in the forest-depths of this far western wilderness, called Dummer? Ten years ago, it might not inaptly have been termed "The *last* clearing in the world." Nor to this day do I know of any in that direction which extends beyond it. Our bush-farm was situated on the border-line of a neighbouring township, only one degree less wild, less out of the world, or nearer to the habitations of civilization than the far-famed "English Line," the boast and glory of this *terra incognita*.

This place, so named by the emigrants who had pitched their tents in that solitary wilderness, was a long line of cleared land, extending upon either side for some miles through the darkest and most interminable forest. The English Line was inhabited chiefly by Cornish miners, who, tired of burrowing like moles underground, had determined to emigrate to Canada, where they could breathe the fresh air of heaven, and obtain the necessaries of life upon the bosom of their mother earth. Strange as it may appear, these men made good farmers, and steady, industrious colonists, working as well above ground as they had toiled in their early days beneath it. All our best servants came from Dummer; and although they spoke a language difficult to be understood, and were uncouth in their manners and appearance, they were faithful and obedient, performing the tasks assigned to them with patient perseverance; good food and kind treatment rendering them always cheerful and contented.

My dear old Jenny, that most faithful and attached of all humble domestic friends, came from Dummer, and I was wont to regard it with complacency for her sake. But Jenny was not English; she was a generous, warm-hearted daughter of the Green Isle—the emerald gem set in the silver of ocean. Yes, Jenny was one of the poorest children of that impoverished but glorious country where wit and talent seem indigenous, springing up spontaneously in the rudest and most uncultivated minds; showing what the land could bring forth in its own strength, unaided by education, and unfettered by the conventional rules of society. Jenny was a striking instance of the worth, noble self-denial, and devotion, which are often met with—and, alas! but too often disregarded—in the poor and ignorant natives of that deeply-injured and much-abused land. A few words about my old favourite may not prove uninteresting to my readers.

Jenny Buchanan, or, as she called it, Bohánon, was the daughter of a petty exciseman, of Scotch extraction (hence her industry), who, at the time of her birth, resided near the old town of Inniskillen. Her mother died a few months after she was born; and her father, within the twelve months, married again. In the mean while the poor orphan babe had been adopted by a kind neighbour, the wife of a small farmer in the vicinity.

In return for coarse food and scanty clothing, the little Jenny became a servant of all work. She fed the pigs, herded the cattle, assisted in planting potatoes and digging peat from the bog, and was undisputed mistress of the poultry-yard. As she grew up to womanhood, the importance of her labours increased. A better reaper in the harvest-field, or footer of turf in the bog, could not be found in the district, or a woman more thoroughly acquainted with the management of cows and the rearing of young cattle; but here poor Jenny's accomplishments terminated.

Her usefulness was all abroad. Within the house she made more dirt than she had the inclination or the ability to clear away. She could neither read, nor knit, nor sew; and although she called herself a Protestant, and a Church of England woman, she knew no more of religion, as revealed to man through the Word of God, than the savage who sinks to the grave in ignorance of a Redeemer. Hence she stoutly resisted all idea of being a sinner, or of standing the least chance of receiving hereafter the condemnation of one.

"Och, shure thin," she would say, with simple earnestness of look and manner, almost irresistible, "God will never throuble Himsel' about a poor, hard-working crathur like me, who never did any harm to the manest of His makin'."

One thing was certain, that a benevolent Providence had "throubled Himsel'" about poor Jenny in times past, for the warm heart of this neglected child of Nature contained a stream of the richest benevolence, which, situated as she had been, could not have been derived from any other source. Honest, faithful, and industrious, Jenny became a law unto herself, and practically illustrated the golden rule of her blessed Lord, "to do unto others as we would they should do unto us." She thought it was impossible that her poor services could ever repay the debt of gratitude that she owed to the family who had brought her up, although the obligation must have been entirely on their side. To them she was greatly attached—for them she toiled unceasingly; and when evil days came, and they were not able to meet the rent-day, or to occupy the farm, she determined to accompany them in their emigration to Canada, and formed one of the stout-hearted band that fixed its location in the lonely and unexplored wilds now known as the township of Dummer.

During the first year of their settlement, the means of obtaining the common necessaries of life became so precarious, that, in order to assist her friends with a little ready money, Jenny determined to hire out into some wealthy house as a servant. When I use the term wealth as applied to any bush-settler, it is of course only comparatively; but Jenny was anxious to obtain a place with settlers who enjoyed a small income independent of their forest means.

Her first speculation was a complete failure. For five long, hopeless years she served a master from whom she never received a farthing of her stipulated wages. Still her attachment to the family was so strong, and had become so much the necessity of her life, that the poor creature could not make up her mind to leave them. The children whom she had received into her arms at their birth, and whom she had nursed with maternal tenderness, were as dear to her as if they had been her own; she continued to work for them, although her clothes were worn to tatters, and her own friends were too poor to replace them.

Her master, Captain N——, a handsome, dashing officer, who had served many years in India, still maintained the carriage and appearance of a gentleman, in spite of his mental and moral degradation, arising from a constant state of intoxication; he still promised to remunerate at some future day her faithful services; and although all his neighbours well knew that his means were exhausted, and that that day would never come, yet Jenny, in the simplicity of her faith, still toiled on, in the hope that the better day he spoke of would soon arrive.

And now a few words respecting this master, which I trust may serve as a warning to others. Allured by the bait that has been the ruin of so many of his class, the offer of a large grant of land, Captain N—— had been induced to form a settlement in this remote and untried township; laying out much, if not all, of his available means in building a log house, and clearing a large extent of barren and stony land. To this uninviting home he conveyed a beautiful young wife, and a small and increasing family. The result may be easily anticipated. The want of society—a dreadful want to a man of his previous habits—the total absence of all the comforts and decencies of life, produced inaction, apathy, and at last, despondency, which was only alleviated by a constant and immoderate use of ardent spirits. As long as Captain N—— retained his half pay, he contrived to exist. In an evil hour he parted with this, and quickly trod the down-hill path to ruin.

And here I would remark that it is always a rash and hazardous step for any officer to part with his half pay; although it is almost every day done, and generally followed by the same disastrous results. A certain income, however small, in a country where money is so hard to be procured, and where labour cannot be attained but at a very high pecuniary remuneration, is invaluable to a gentleman unaccustomed to agricultural employment; who, without this reserve to pay his people, during the brief but expensive seasons of seed-time and harvest, must either work himself or starve. I have known no instance in which such sale has been attended with ultimate advantage; but, alas! too many in which it has terminated in the most distressing destitution. These government grants of land, to half-pay officers, have induced numbers of this class to emigrate to the backwoods of Canada, who are totally unfit for pioneers; but, tempted by the offer of finding themselves landholders of what, on paper, appear to them fine estates, they resign a certainty, to waste their energies, and die half-starved and broken-hearted in the depths of the pitiless wild.

If a gentleman so situated would give up all idea of settling on his grant, but hire a good farm in a favourable situation—that is, not too far from a market—and with his half pay hire efficient labourers, of which plenty are now to be had, to cultivate the land, with common prudence and economy, he would soon obtain a comfortable subsistence for his family. And if the males were brought up to share the burden and heat of the day, the expense of hired labour, as it yearly diminished, would add to the general means and well-being of the whole, until the hired farm became the real property of the industrious tenants. But the love of show, the vain boast of appearing richer and better dressed than our neighbours, too often involves the emigrant's family in debt, from which they are seldom able to extricate themselves without sacrificing the means which would have secured their independence.

This, although a long digression, will not, I hope, be without its use; and if this book is regarded not as a work of amusement but one of practical experience, written for the benefit of others, it will not fail to convey some useful hints to those who have contemplated emigration to Canada: the best country in the world for the industrious and well-principled man, who really comes out to work, and to better his condition by the labour of his hands; but a gulf of ruin to the vain and idle, who only set foot upon these shores to accelerate their ruin.

But to return to Captain N——. It was at this disastrous period that Jenny entered his service. Had her master adapted his habits and expenditure to his altered circumstances, much misery might have been spared, both to himself and his family. But he was a proud man—too proud to work, or to receive with kindness the offers of service tendered to him by his half-civilized, but well-meaning neighbours.

"Hang him!" cried an indignant English settler (Captain N—— was an Irishman), whose offer of drawing wood had been rejected with unmerited contempt. "Wait a few years and we shall see what his pride will do for him. *I am* sorry for his poor wife and children; but for himself, I have no pity for him."

This man had been uselessly insulted, at the very moment when he was anxious to perform a kind and benevolent action; when, like a true Englishman, his heart was softened by witnessing the sufferings of a young delicate female and her infant family. Deeply affronted by the Captain's foolish conduct, he now took a malignant pleasure in watching his arrogant neighbour's progress to ruin.

The year after the sale of his commission, Captain N—— found himself considerably in debt, "Never mind, Ella," he said to his anxious wife; "the crops will pay all."

The crops were a failure that year. Creditors pressed hard; the Captain had no money to pay his workmen, and he would not work himself. Disgusted with his location, but unable to change it for a better; without friends of his own class (for he was the only gentleman then resident in the new township), to relieve the monotony of his existence with their society, or to afford him advice or assistance in his difficulties, the fatal whiskey-bottle became his refuge from gloomy thoughts.

His wife, an amiable and devoted creature, well born, well educated, and deserving of a better lot, did all in her power to wean him from the growing vice. But, alas! the pleadings of an angel, in such circumstances, would have had little effect upon the mind of such a man. He loved her as well as he could love any thing, and he fancied that he loved his children, while he was daily reducing them, by his favourite vice, to beggary.

For awhile, he confined his excesses to his own fireside, but this was only for as long a period as the sale of his stock and land would supply him with the means of criminal indulgence. After a time, all these resources failed, and his large grant of eight hundred acres of land had been converted into whiskey, except the one hundred acres on which his house and barn stood, embracing the small clearing from which the family derived their scanty supply of wheat and potatoes. For the sake of peace, his wife gave up all her ornaments and household plate, and the best articles of a once handsome and ample wardrobe, in the hope of hiding her sorrows from the world, and keeping her husband at home.

The pride, that had rendered him so obnoxious to his humbler neighbours, yielded at length to the inordinate craving for drink; the man who had held himself so high above his honest and industrious fellow-settlers, could now unblushingly enter their cabins and beg for a drop of whiskey. The feeling of shame once subdued, there was no end to his audacious mendicity. His whole time was spent in wandering about the country, calling upon every new settler, in the hope of being asked to partake of the coveted poison. He was even known to enter by the window of an emigrant's cabin, during the absence of the owner, and remain drinking in the house while a drop of spirits could be found in the cupboard. When driven forth by the angry owner of the hut, he wandered on to the distant town of P——, and lived there in a low tavern, while his wife and children were starving at home.

"He is the filthiest beast in the township," said the aforementioned neighbour to me; "it would be a good thing for his wife and children if his worthless neck were broken in one of his drunken sprees."

This might be the melancholy fact, but it was not the less dreadful on that account. The husband of an affectionate wife—the father of a lovely family—and his death to be a matter of rejoicing!—a blessing, instead of being an affliction!—an agony not to be thought upon without the deepest sorrow.

It was at this melancholy period of her sad history that Mrs. N—— found, in Jenny Buchanan, a help in her hour of need. The heart of the faithful creature bled for the misery which involved the wife of her degraded master, and the children she so dearly loved. Their want and destitution called all the sympathies of her ardent nature into active operation; they were long indebted to her labour for every morsel of food which they consumed. For them, she sowed, she planted, she reaped. Every block of wood which shed a cheering warmth around their desolate home was cut from the forest by her own hands, and brought up a steep hill to the house upon her back. For them, she coaxed the neighbours, with whom she was a general favourite, out of many a mess of eggs for their especial benefit; while with her cheerful songs, and hearty, hopeful disposition, she dispelled much of the cramping despair which chilled the heart of the unhappy mother in her deserted home.

For several years did this great, poor woman keep the wolf from the door of her beloved mistress, toiling for her with the strength and energy of a man. When was man ever so devoted, so devoid of all selfishness, so attached to employers, yet poorer than herself, as this uneducated Irishwoman?

A period was at length put to her unrequited services. In a fit of intoxication her master beat her severely with the iron ramrod of his gun, and turned her, with abusive language, from his doors. Oh, hard return for all her unpaid labours of love! She forgave this outrage for the sake of the helpless beings who depended upon her care. He repeated the injury, and the poor creature returned almost heart-broken to her former home.

Thinking that his spite would subside in a few days, Jenny made a third effort to enter his house in her usual capacity; but Mrs. N—— told her, with many tears, that her presence would only enrage her husband, who had threatened herself with the most cruel treatment if she allowed the faithful servant again to enter the house. Thus ended her five years' service to this ungrateful master. Such was her reward!

I heard of Jenny's worth and kindness from the Englishman who had been so grievously affronted by Captain N——, and sent for her to come to me. She instantly accepted my offer, and returned with my messenger. She had scarcely a garment to cover her. I was obliged to find her a suit of clothes before I could set her to work. The smiles and dimples of my curly-headed, rosy little Donald, then a baby-boy of fifteen months, consoled the old woman for her separation from Ellie N——; and the good-will with which all the children (now four in number) regarded the kind old body, soon endeared to her the new home which Providence had assigned to her.

Her accounts of Mrs. N——, and her family, soon deeply interested me in her fate; and Jenny never went to visit her friends in Dummer without an interchange of good wishes passing between us.

The year of the Canadian rebellion came, and brought with it sorrow into many a bush dwelling. Old Jenny and I were left alone with the little children, in the depths of the dark forest, to help ourselves in the best way we could. Men could not be procured in that thinly-settled spot for love nor money, and I now fully realized the extent of Jenny's usefulness. Daily she yoked the oxen, and brought down from the bush fuel to maintain our fires, which she felled and chopped up with her own hands. She fed the cattle, and kept all things snug about the doors; not forgetting to load her master's two guns, "in case," as she said, "the ribels should attack us in our retrate."

The months of November and December of 1838 had been unnaturally mild for this iron climate; but the opening of the ensuing January brought a short but severe spell of frost and snow. We felt very lonely in our solitary dwelling, crouching round the blazing fire, that scarcely chased the cold from our miserable log tenement, until this dreary period was suddenly cheered by the unexpected presence of my beloved friend, Emilia, who came to spend a week with me in my forest home.

She brought her own baby-boy with her, and an ample supply of buffalo robes, not forgetting a treat of baker's bread, and "sweeties" for the children. Oh, dear Emilia! best and kindest of women, though absent in your native land, long, long shall my heart cherish with affectionate gratitude all your visits of love, and turn to you as to a sister, tried, and found most faithful, in the dark hour of adversity, and amidst the almost total neglect of those from whom nature claimed a tenderer and holier sympathy.

Great was the joy of Jenny at this accession to our family party; and after Mrs. S—— was well warmed, and had partaken of tea—the only refreshment we could offer her—we began to talk over the news of the place.

"By the by, Jenny," said she, turning to the old servant, who was undressing the little boy by the fire, "have you heard lately from poor Mrs. N——? We have been told that she and the family are in a dreadful state of destitution. That worthless man has left them for the States, and it is supposed that he has joined Mackenzie's band of ruffians on Navy Island; but whether this be true or false, he has deserted his wife and children, taking his eldest son along with him (who might have been of some service at home), and leaving them without money or food."

"The good Lord! What will become of the crathurs?" responded Jenny, wiping her wrinkled cheek with the back of her hard, brown hand. "An' thin they have not a sowl to chop and draw them firewood; an' the weather so oncommon savare. Och hone! what has not that *baste* of a man to answer for?"

"I heard," continued Mrs. S——, "that they have tasted no food but potatoes for the last nine months, and scarcely enough of them to keep soul and body together; that they have sold their last cow; and the poor young lady and her second brother, a lad of only twelve years old, bring all the wood for the fire from the bush on a hand-sleigh."

"Oh, dear!—oh, dear!" sobbed Jenny; "an' I not there to hilp them! An' poor Miss Mary, the tinder thing! Oh, 'tis hard, terribly hard for the crathurs! an' they not used to the like."

"Can nothing be done for them?" said I.

"That is what we want to know," returned Emilia, "and that was one of my reasons for coming up to D——. I wanted to consult you and Jenny upon the subject. You, who are an officer's wife, and I, who am both an officer's wife and daughter, ought to devise some plan of rescuing this unfortunate lady and her family from her present forlorn situation."

The tears sprang to my eyes, and I thought, in the bitterness of my heart, upon my own galling poverty, that my pockets did not contain even a single copper, and that I had scarcely garments enough to shield me from the inclemency of the weather. By unflinching industry, and taking my part in the toil of the field, I had bread for myself and family, and this was more than poor Mrs. N—— possessed; but it appeared impossible for me to be of any assistance to the unhappy sufferer, and the thought of my incapacity gave me severe pain. It was only in moments like the present that I felt the curse of poverty.

"Well," continued my friend, "you see, Mrs. Moodie, that the ladies of P—— are all anxious to do what they can for her; but they first want to learn if the miserable circumstances in which she is said to be placed are true. In short, my dear friend, they want you and me to make a pilgrimage to Dummer, to see the poor lady herself; and then they will be guided by our report."

"Then let us lose no time in going upon our own mission of mercy."

"Och, my dear heart, you will be lost in the woods!" said old Jenny. "It is nine long miles to the first clearing, and that through a lonely, blazed path. After you are through the beaver-meadow, there is not a single hut for you to rest or warm yourselves. It is too much for the both of yees; you will be frozen to death on the road."

"No fear," said my benevolent friend; "God will take care of us, Jenny. It is on His errand we go; to carry a message of hope to one about to perish."

"The Lord bless you for a darlint," cried the old woman, devoutly kissing the velvet cheek of the little fellow sleeping upon her lap. "May your own purty child never know the want and sorrow that is around her."

Emilia and I talked over the Dummer scheme until we fell asleep. Many were the plans we proposed for the immediate relief of the unfortunate family. Early the next morning, my brother-in-law, Mr. T——, called upon my friend. The subject next our heart was immediately introduced, and he was called into the general council. His feelings, like our own, were deeply interested; and he proposed that we should each provide something from our own small stores to satisfy the pressing wants of the distressed family; while he promised to bring his cutter the next morning, and take us through the beaver-meadow, and to the edge of the great swamp, which would shorten four miles, at least, of our long and hazardous journey.

We joyfully acceded to his proposal, and set cheerfully to work to provide for the morrow. Jenny baked a batch of her very best bread, and boiled a large piece of beef; and Mr. T—— brought with him, the next day, a fine cooked ham, in a sack, into the bottom of which he stowed the beef and loaves, besides some sugar and tea, which his own kind wife, the author of "The Backwoods of Canada," had sent. I had some misgivings as to the manner in which these good things could be introduced to the poor lady, who, I had heard, was reserved and proud.

"Oh, Jenny," I said, "how shall I be able to ask her to accept provisions from strangers? I am afraid of wounding her feelings."

"Oh, darlint, never fear that! She is proud, I know; but 'tis not a stiff pride, but jist enough to consale her disthress from her ignorant English neighbours, who think so manely of poor folk like her who were once rich. She will be very thankful to you for your kindness, for she has not experienced much of it from the Dummer people in her throuble, though she may have no words to tell you so. Say that old Jenny sent the bread to dear wee Ellie, 'cause she knew she would like a loaf of Jenny's bakin'."

"But the meat."

"Och, the mate, is it? Maybe, you'll think of some excuse for the mate when you get there."

"I hope so; but I'm a sad coward with strangers, and I

have lived so long out of the world that I am at a great loss what to do. I will try and put a good face on the matter. Your name, Jenny, will be no small help to me."

All was now ready. Kissing our little bairns, who crowded around us with eager and inquiring looks, and charging Jenny for the hundredth time to take especial care of them during our absence, we mounted the cutter, and set off, under the care and protection of Mr. T——, who determined to accompany us on the journey.

It was a black, cold day; no sun visible in the gray, dark sky; a keen, cutting wind, and hard frost. We crouched close to each other.

"Good heavens, how cold it is!" whispered Emilia. "What a day for such a journey!"

She had scarcely ceased speaking, when the cutter went upon a stump which lay concealed under the drifted snow; and we, together with the ruins of our conveyance, were scattered around.

"A bad beginning," said my brother-in-law, with a rueful aspect, as he surveyed the wreck of the cutter from which we had promised ourselves so much benefit. "There is no help for it but to return home."

"Oh, no," said Mrs. S——; "bad beginnings make good endings, you know. Let us go on; it will be far better walking than riding such a dreadful day. My feet are half frozen already with sitting still."

"But, my dear madam," expostulated Mr. T——, "consider the distance, the road, the dark, dull day, and our imperfect knowledge of the path. I will get the cutter mended to-morrow; and the day after we may be able to proceed."

"Delays are dangerous," said the pertinacious Emilia, who, woman-like, was determined to have her own way. "Now, or never. While we wait for the broken cutter, the broken-hearted Mrs. N—— may starve. We can stop at Colonel C——'s and warm ourselves, and you can leave the cutter at his house until our return."

"It was upon your account that I proposed the delay," said the good Mr. T——, taking the sack, which was no inconsiderable weight, upon his shoulder, and driving his horse before him into neighbour W——'s stable. "Where you go, I am ready to follow."

When we arrived, Colonel C——'s family were at breakfast, of which they made us partake; and after vainly endeavouring to dissuade us from what appeared to them our Quixotic expedition, Mrs. C—— added a dozen fine white fish to the contents of the sack, and sent her youngest son to help Mr. T—— along with his burthen, and to bear us company on our desolate road.

Leaving the Colonel's hospitable house on our left, we again plunged into the woods, and after a few minutes' brisk walking, found ourselves upon the brow of a steep bank that overlooked the beaver-meadow, containing within its area several hundred acres.

There is no scenery in the bush that presents such a novel appearance as those meadows, or openings, surrounded, as they invariably are, by dark, intricate forests; their high, rugged banks covered with the light, airy tamarack and silver birch. In summer they look like a lake of soft, rich verdure, hidden in the bosom of the barren and howling waste. Lakes they certainly have been, from which the waters have receded, "ages, ages long ago;" and still the whole length of these curious level valleys is traversed by a stream, of no inconsiderable dimensions.

The waters of the narrow, rapid creek, which flowed through the meadow we were about to cross, were of sparkling brightness, and icy cold. The frost-king had no power to check their swift, dancing movements, or stop their perpetual song. On they leaped, sparkling and flashing beneath their ice-crowned banks, rejoicing as they revelled on in their lonely course. In the prime of the year, this is a wild and lovely spot, the grass is of the richest green, and the flowers of the most gorgeous dyes. The gayest butterflies float above them upon painted wings; and the whip-poor-will pours forth from the neighbouring woods, at close of dewy eve, his strange but sadly plaintive cry. Winter was now upon the earth, and the once green meadow looked like a small forest lake covered with snow.

The first step we made into it plunged us up to the knees in the snow, which was drifted to a great height in the open space. Mr. T—— and our young friend C—— walked on ahead of us, in order to break a track through the untrodden snow. We soon reached the cold creek; but here a new difficulty presented itself. It was too wide to jump across, and we could see no other way of passing to the other side.

"There must be some sort of a bridge hereabout," said young C——, "or how can the people from Dummer pass constantly during the winter to and fro. I will go along the bank, and halloo to you if I find one."

In a few minutes he gave the desired signal, and on reaching the spot, we found a round, slippery log flung across the stream by way of bridge. With some trouble, and after various slips, we got safely on the other side. To wet our feet would have been to ensure their being frozen; and as it was, we were not without serious apprehensions on that score. After crossing the bleak, snowy plain, we scrambled over another brook, and entered the great swamp, which occupied two miles of our dreary road.

It would be vain to attempt giving any description of this tangled maze of closely-interwoven cedars, fallen trees, and loose-scattered masses of rock. It seemed the fitting abode of wolves and bears, and every other unclean beast. The fire had run through it during the summer, making the confusion doubly confused. Now we stopped, half doubled, to crawl under fallen branches that hung over our path, then again we had to clamber over prostrate trees of great bulk, descending from which we plumped down into holes in the snow, sinking mid-leg into the rotten trunk of some treacherous, decayed pine-tree. Before we were half through the great swamp, we began to think ourselves sad fools, and to wish that we were safe again by our own firesides. But, then, a great object was in view,—the relief of a distressed fellow-creature, and like the "full of hope, misnamed forlorn," we determined to overcome every difficulty, and toil on.

It took us an hour at least to clear the great swamp, from which we emerged into a fine wood, composed chiefly of maple-trees. The sun had, during our immersion in the dark shades of the swamp, burst through his leaden shroud, and cast a cheery gleam along the rugged boles of the lofty trees. The squirrel and chissmunk occasionally bounded across our path; the dazzling snow which covered it reflected the branches above us in an endless variety of dancing shadows. Our spirits rose in proportion. Young C—— burst out singing, and Emilia and I laughed and chatted as we bounded along our narrow road. On, on for hours, the same interminable forest stretched away to the right and left, before and behind us.

"It is past twelve," said my brother T——, thoughtfully; "if we do not soon come to a clearing, we may chance to spend the night in the forest.

"Oh, I am dying with hunger," cried Emilia. "Do, C——, give us one or two of the cakes your mother put into the bag for us to eat upon the road."

The ginger-cakes were instantly produced. But where were the teeth to be found that could masticate them? The cakes were frozen as hard as stones; this was a great disappointment to us tired and hungry wights; but it only produced a hearty laugh. Over the logs we went again; for it was a perpetual stepping up and down, crossing the fallen trees that obstructed our path. At last we came to a spot where two distinct blazed roads diverged.

"What are we to do now?" said Mr. T——.

We stopped, and a general consultation was held, and without one dissenting voice we took the branch to the right, which, after pursuing for about half-a-mile, led us to a log hut of the rudest description.

"Is this the road to Dummer?" we asked a man, who was chopping wood outside the fence.

"I guess you are in Dummer?" was the answer.

My heart leaped for joy, for I was dreadfully fatigued.

"Does this road lead through the English Line?"

"That's another thing," returned the woodman. "No; you turned off from the right path when you came up here." We all looked very blank at each other. "You will have to go back, and keep the other road, and that will lead you straight to the English Line."

"How many miles is it to Mrs. N——'s?"

"Some four, or thereabouts," was the cheering rejoinder. "'Tis one of the last clearings on the line. If you are going back to Douro to-night, you must look sharp."

Sadly and dejectedly we retraced our steps. There are few trifling failures more bitter in our journey through life than that of a tired traveller mistaking his road. What effect must that tremendous failure produce upon the human mind, when, at the end of life's unretraceable journey, the traveller finds that he has fallen upon the wrong track through every stage, and instead of arriving at the land of blissful promise, sinks for ever into the gulf of despair!

The distance we had trodden in the wrong path, while led on by hope and anticipation, now seemed to double in length, as with painful steps we toiled on to reach the right road. This object once attained, soon led us to the dwellings of men.

Neat, comfortable log houses, surrounded by well-fenced patches of clearing, arose on either side of the forest road; dogs flew out and barked at us, and children ran shouting in-doors to tell their respective owners that strangers were passing their gates; a most unusual circumstance, I should think, in that location.

A servant who had hired two years with my brother-in-law, we knew must live somewhere in this neighbourhood, at whose fireside we hoped not only to rest and warm ourselves, but to obtain something to eat. On going up to one of the cabins to inquire for Hannah J——, we fortunately happened to light upon the very person we sought. With many exclamations of surprise, she ushered us into her neat and comfortable log dwelling.

A blazing fire, composed of two huge logs, was roaring up the wide chimney, and the savoury smell that issued from a large pot of pea-soup was very agreeable to our cold and hungry stomachs. But, alas, the refreshment went no further! Hannah most politely begged us to take seats by the fire, and warm and rest ourselves; she even knelt down and assisted in rubbing our half-frozen hands; but she never once made mention of the hot soup, or of the tea, which was drawing in a tin tea-pot upon the hearth-stone, or of a glass of whiskey, which would have been thankfully accepted by our male pilgrims.

Hannah was not an Irishwoman, no, nor a Scotch lassie, or her very first request would have been for us to take "a pickle of soup," or "a sup of thae warm broths." The soup was no doubt cooking for Hannah's husband and two neighbours, who were chopping for him in the bush; and whose want of punctuality she feelingly lamented.

As we left her cottage, and jogged on, Emilia whispered, laughing, "I hope you are satisfied with your good dinner? Was not the pea-soup excellent?—and that cup of nice hot tea!—I never relished any thing more in my life. I think we should never pass that house without giving Hannah a call, and testifying our gratitude for her good cheer."

Many times did we stop to inquire the way to Mrs. N——'s, before we ascended the steep, bleak hill upon which her house stood. At the door, Mr. T—— deposited the sack of provisions, and he and young C—— went across the road to the house of an English settler (who, fortunately for them, proved more hospitable than Hannah J——), to wait until our errand was executed.

The house before which Emilia and I were standing had once been a tolerably comfortable log dwelling. It was larger than such buildings generally are, and was surrounded by dilapidated barns and stables, which were not cheered by a solitary head of cattle. A black pine forest stretched away to the north of the house, and terminated in a dismal, tangled cedar swamp, the entrance to the house not having been constructed to face the road.

The spirit that had borne me up during the journey died within me. I was fearful that my visit would be deemed an impertinent intrusion. I knew not in what manner to introduce myself, and my embarrassment had been greatly increased by Mrs. S—— declaring that I must break the ice, for she had not courage to go in. I remonstrated, but she was firm. To hold any longer parley was impossible. We were standing on the top of a bleak hill, with the thermometer many degrees below zero, and exposed to the fiercest biting of the bitter, cutting blast. With a heavy sigh, I knocked slowly but decidedly at the crazy door. I saw the curly head of a boy glance for a moment against the broken window. There was a stir within, but no one answered our summons. Emilia was rubbing her hands together, and beating a rapid tattoo with her feet upon the hard and glittering snow, to keep them from freezing.

Again I appealed to the inhospitable door, with a vehemence which seemed to say, "We are freezing, good people; in mercy let us in!"

Again there was a stir, and a whispered sound of voices, as if in consultation, from within; and after waiting a few minutes longer—which, cold as we were, seemed an age—the door was cautiously opened by a handsome, dark-eyed lad of twelve years of age, who was evidently the owner of the curly head that had been sent to reconnoitre us through the window. Carefully closing the door after him, he stepped out upon the snow, and asked us coldly but respectfully what we wanted. I told him that we were two ladies, who had walked all the way from Douro to see his mamma, and that we wished very much to speak to her. The lad answered us, with the ease and courtesy of a gentleman, that he did not know whether his mamma could be seen by strangers, but he would go in and see. So saying he abruptly left us, leaving behind him an ugly skeleton of a dog, who, after expressing his disapprobation at our presence in the most disagreeable and unequivocal manner, pounced like a famished wolf upon the sack of good things which lay at Emilia's feet; and our united efforts could scarcely keep him off.

"A cold, doubtful reception, this!" said my friend, turning her back to the wind, and hiding her face in her muff. "This is worse than Hannah's liberality, and the long, weary walk."

I thought so too, and began to apprehend that our walk had been in vain, when the lad again appeared, and said that we might walk in, for his mother was dressed.

Emilia, true to her determination, went no farther than the passage. In vain were all my entreating looks and mute appeals to her benevolence and friendship; I was forced to enter alone the apartment that contained the distressed family.

I felt that I was treading upon sacred ground, for a pitying angel hovers over the abode of suffering virtue, and hallows all its woes. On a rude bench, before the fire, sat a lady, between thirty and forty years of age, dressed in a thin, coloured muslin gown, the most inappropriate garment for the rigour of the season, but, in all probability, the only decent one that she retained. A subdued melancholy looked forth from her large, dark, pensive eyes. She appeared like one who, having discovered the full extent of her misery, had proudly steeled her heart to bear it. Her countenance was very pleasing, and, in early life (but she was still young), she must have been eminently handsome. Near her, with her head bent down, and shaded by her thin, slender hand, her slight figure scarcely covered by her scanty clothing, sat her eldest daughter, a gentle, sweet-looking girl, who held in her arms a baby brother, whose destitution she endeavoured to conceal. It was a touching sight; that suffering girl, just stepping into womanhood, hiding against her young bosom the nakedness of the little creature she loved. Another fine boy, whose neatly-patched clothes had not one piece of the original stuff apparently left in them, stood behind his mother, with dark, glistening eyes fastened upon me, as if amused, and wondering who I was, and what business I could have there. A pale and attenuated, but very pretty, delicately-featured little girl was seated on a low stool before the fire.

This was old Jenny's darling, Ellie, or Eloise. A rude bedstead, of home manufacture, in a corner of the room, covered with a coarse woollen quilt, contained two little boys, who had crept into it to conceal their wants from the eyes of the stranger. On the table lay a dozen peeled potatoes, and a small pot was boiling on the fire, to receive this their scanty and only daily meal. There was such an air of patient and enduring suffering in the whole group, that, as I gazed heart-stricken upon it, my fortitude quite gave way, and I burst into tears.

Mrs. N—— first broke the painful silence, and, rather proudly, asked me to whom she had the pleasure of speaking. I made a desperate effort to regain my composure, and told her, but with much embarrassment, my name; adding that I was so well acquainted with her and her children, through Jenny, that I could not consider her as a stranger; that I hoped that, as I was the wife of an officer, and, like her, a resident in the bush, and well acquainted with all its trials and privations, she would look upon me as a friend.

She seemed surprised and annoyed, and I found no small difficulty in introducing the object of my visit; but the day was rapidly declining, and I knew that not a moment was to be lost. At first she coldly rejected all offers of service, and said that she was contented, and wanted for nothing.

I appealed to the situation in which I beheld herself and her children, and implored her, for their sakes, not to refuse help from friends who felt for her distress. Her maternal feelings triumphed over her assumed indifference, and when she saw me weeping, for I could no longer restrain my tears, her pride yielded, and for some minutes not a word was spoken. I heard the large tears, as they slowly fell from her daughter's eyes, drop one by one upon her garments.

At last the poor girl sobbed out, "Dear mamma, why conceal the truth? You know that we are nearly naked, and starving."

Then came the sad tale of domestic woes:—the absence of the husband and eldest son; the uncertainty as to where they were, or in what engaged; the utter want of means to procure the common necessaries of life; the sale of the only remaining cow that used to provide the children with food. It had been sold for twelve dollars, part to be paid in cash, part in potatoes; the potatoes were nearly exhausted, and they were allowanced to so many a day. But the six dollars she had retained as their last resource. Alas! she had sent the eldest boy the day before to P——, to get a letter out of the post-office, which she hoped contained some tidings of her husband and son. She was all anxiety and expectation—but the child returned late at night without the letter which they had longed for with such feverish impatience. The six dollars upon which they had depended for a supply of food were in notes of the Farmer's Bank, which at that time would not pass for money, and which the roguish purchaser of the cow had passed off upon this distressed family.

Oh! imagine, ye who revel in riches—who can daily throw away a large sum upon the merest toy—the cruel disappointment, the bitter agony of this poor mother's heart, when she received this calamitous news, in the midst of her starving children. For the last nine weeks they had lived upon a scanty supply of potatoes;—they had not tasted raised bread or animal food for eighteen months.

"Ellie," said I, anxious to introduce the sack, which had lain like a nightmare upon my mind, "I have something for you; Jenny baked some loaves last night, and sent them to you with her best love."

The eyes of all the children grew bright. "You will find the sack with the bread in the passage," said I to one of the boys. He rushed joyfully out, and returned with Mrs. —— and the sack. Her bland and affectionate greeting restored us all to tranquillity.

The delighted boy opened the sack. The first thing he produced was the ham.

"Oh," said I, "that is a ham that my sister sent to Mrs. N——; 'tis of her own curing, and she thought that it might be acceptable."

Then came the white fish, nicely packed in a clean cloth. "Mrs. C—— thought fish might be a treat to Mrs. N——, as she lived so far from the great lakes." Then came Jenny's bread, which had already been introduced. The beef, and tea, and sugar, fell upon the floor without any comment. The first scruples had been overcome, and the day was ours.

"And now, ladies," said Mrs. N——, with true hospitality, "since you have brought refreshments with you, permit me to cook something for your dinner."

The scene I had just witnessed had produced such a choking sensation that all my hunger had vanished. Before we could accept or refuse Mrs. N——'s kind offer, Mr. T—— arrived, to hurry us off.

It was two o'clock when we descended the hill in front of the house, that led by a side-path round to the road, and commenced our homeward route. I thought the four miles of clearings would never be passed; and the English Line appeared to have no end. At length we entered once more the dark forest.

The setting sun gleamed along the ground; the necessity of exerting our utmost speed, and getting through the great swamp before darkness surrounded us, was apparent to all. The men strode vigorously forward, for they had been refreshed with a substantial dinner of potatoes and pork, washed down with a glass of whiskey, at the cottage in which they had waited for us; but poor Emilia and I, faint, hungry, and foot-sore, it was with the greatest difficulty we could keep up. I thought of Rosalind, as our march up and down the fallen logs recommenced, and often exclaimed with her, "Oh, Jupiter! how weary are my legs!"

Night closed in just as we reached the beaver-meadow. Here our ears were greeted with the sound of well-known voices. James and Henry C—— had brought the ox-sleigh to meet us at the edge of the bush. Never was splendid equipage greeted with such delight. Emilia and I, now fairly exhausted with fatigue, scrambled into it, and lying down on the straw which covered the bottom of the rude vehicle, we drew the buffalo robes over our faces, and actually slept soundly until we reached Colonel C——'s hospitable door.

An excellent supper of hot fish and fried venison was smoking on the table, with other good cheer, to which we did ample justice. I, for one, was never so hungry in my life. We had fasted for twelve hours, and that on an intensely cold day, and had walked during that period upwards of twenty miles. Never, never shall I forget that weary walk to Dummer; but a blessing followed it.

It was midnight when Emilia and I reached my humble home; our good friends the oxen being again put in requisition to carry us there. Emilia went immediately to bed, from which she was unable to rise for several days. In the mean while I wrote to Moodie an account of the scene I had witnessed, and he raised a subscription among the officers of the regiment for the poor lady and her children, which amounted to forty dollars. Emilia lost no time in making a full report to her friends at P——; and before a week passed away, Mrs. N—— and her family were removed thither by several benevolent individuals in the place. A neat cottage was hired for her; and, to the honour of Canada be it spoken, all who could afford a donation gave cheerfully. Farmers left at her door, pork, beef, flour, and potatoes; the storekeepers sent groceries, and goods to make clothes for the children; the shoemakers contributed boots for the boys; while the ladies did all in their power to assist and comfort the gentle creature thus thrown by Providence upon their bounty.

While Mrs. N—— remained at P—— she did not want for any comfort. Her children were clothed and her rent paid by her benevolent friends, and her house supplied with food and many comforts from the same source. Respected and beloved by all who knew her, it would have been well had she never left the quiet asylum where, for several years, she enjoyed tranquillity, and a respectable competence from her school; but in an evil hour she followed her worthless husband to the Southern States, and again suffered all the woes which drunkenness inflicts upon the wives and children of its degraded victims.

# CHAPTER XII.

## A CHANGE IN OUR PROSPECTS.

DURING my illness, a kind neighbour, who had not only frequently come to see me, but had brought me many nourishing things, made by her own fair hands, took a great fancy to my second daughter, who, lively and volatile, could not be induced to remain quiet in the sick chamber. The noise she made greatly retarded my recovery, and Mrs. H—— took her home with her, as the only means of obtaining for me necessary rest. During that winter, and through the ensuing summer, I only received occasional visits from my little girl, who, fairly established with her new friends, looked upon their house as her home.

This separation, which was felt as a great benefit at the time, greatly estranged the affections of the child from her own people. She saw us so seldom that she almost regarded us, when she did meet, as strangers; and I often deeply lamented the hour when I had unwittingly suffered the threefold cord of domestic love to be unravelled by absence, and the flattering attentions which fed the vanity of a beautiful child, without strengthening her moral character. Mrs. H——, whose husband was wealthy, was a generous, warm-hearted girl of eighteen. Lovely in person, and fascinating in manners, and still too young to have any idea of forming the character of a child, she dressed the little creature expensively; and, by constantly praising her personal appearance, gave her an idea of her own importance which it took many years to eradicate.

It is a great error to suffer a child, who has been trained in the hard school of poverty and self-denial, to be transplanted suddenly into the hot-bed of wealth and luxury. The idea of the child being so much happier and better off blinds her fond parents to the dangers of her new situation, where she is sure to contract a dislike to all useful occupation, and to look upon scanty means and plain clothing as a disgrace. If the reaction is bad for a grown-up person, it is almost destructive to a child who is incapable of moral reflection. Whenever I saw little Addie, and remarked the growing coldness of her manner towards us, my heart reproached me for having exposed her to temptation.

Still, in the eye of the world, she was much better situated than she could possibly be with us. The heart of the parent could alone understand the change.

So sensible was her father of this alteration, that the first time he paid us a visit he went and brought home his child.

"If she remain so long away from us, at her tender years," he said, "she will cease to love us. All the wealth in the world would not compensate me for the love of my child."

The removal of my sister rendered my separation from my husband doubly lonely and irksome. Sometimes the desire to see and converse with him would press so painfully on my heart that I would get up in the night, strike a light, and sit down and write him a long letter, and tell him all that was in my mind; and when I had thus unburdened my spirit, the letter was committed to the flames, and after fervently commending him to the care of the Great Father of mankind, I would lay down my throbbing head on my pillow beside our first-born son, and sleep tranquilly.

It is a strange fact that many of my husband's letters to me were written at the very time when I felt those irresistible impulses to hold communion with him. Why should we be ashamed to admit openly our belief in this mysterious intercourse between the spirits of those who are bound to each other by the tender ties of friendship and affection, when the experience of every day proves its truth? Proverbs, which are the wisdom of ages collected into a few brief words, tell us in one pithy sentence that "if we talk of the devil he is sure to appear." While the name of a long-absent friend is in our mouth, the next moment brings him into our presence. How can this be, if mind did not meet mind, and the spirit had not a prophetic consciousness of the vicinity of another spirit, kindred with its own? This is an occurrence so common that I never met with any person to whom it had not happened; few will admit it to be a spiritual agency, but in no other way can they satisfactorily explain its cause. If it were a mere coincidence, or combination of ordinary circumstances, it would not happen so often, and people would not be led to speak of the long absent always at the moment when they are just about to present themselves before them. My husband was no believer in what he termed my fanciful, speculative theories; yet at the time when his youngest boy and myself lay dangerously ill, and hardly expected to live, I received from him a letter, written in great haste, which commenced with this sentence: "Do write to me, dear S——, when you receive this. I have felt very uneasy about you for some days past, and am afraid that all is not right at home."

Whence came this sudden fear? Why at that particular time did his thoughts turn so despondingly towards those so dear to him? Why did the dark cloud in his mind hang so heavily above his home? The burden of my weary and distressed spirit had reached him; and without knowing of our sufferings and danger, his own responded to the call.

The holy and mysterious nature of man is yet hidden from himself; he is still a stranger to the movements of that inner life, and knows little of its capabilities and powers. A purer religion, a higher standard of moral and intellectual training, may in time reveal all this. Man still remains a half-reclaimed savage; the leaven of Christianity is slowly and surely working its way, but it has not yet changed the whole lump, or transformed the deformed into the beauteous child of God. Oh, for that glorious day! It is coming. The dark clouds of humanity are already tinged with the golden radiance of the dawn, but the sun of righteousness has not yet arisen upon the world with healing on his wings; the light of truth still struggles in the womb of darkness, and man stumbles on to the fulfilment of his sublime and mysterious destiny.

This spring I was not a little puzzled how to get in the crops. I still continued so weak that I was quite unable to assist in the field, and my good old Jenny was sorely troubled with inflamed feet, which required constant care. At this juncture, a neighbouring settler, who had recently come among us, offered to put in my small crop of peas, potatoes, and oats, in all not comprising more than eight acres, if I would lend him my oxen to log-up a large fallow of ten acres, and put in his own crops. Trusting to his fair dealing, I consented to this arrangement; but he took advantage of my isolated position, and not only logged-up his fallow, but put in all his spring crops before he sowed an acre of mine. The oxen were worked down so low that they were almost unfit for use, and my crops were put in so late, and with such little care, that they all proved a failure. I should have felt this loss more severely had it happened in any previous year, but I had ceased to feel that deep interest in the affairs of the farm, from a sort of conviction in my own mind that it would not long remain my home.

Jenny and I did our best in the way of hoeing and weeding; but no industry on our part could repair the injury done to the seed by being sown out of season.

We therefore confined our attention to the garden, which, as usual, was very productive, and with milk, fresh butter, and eggs, supplied the simple wants of our family. Emilia enlivened our solitude by her company, for several weeks during the summer, and we had many pleasant excursions on the water together.

My knowledge of the use of the paddle, however, was not entirely without its danger.

One very windy Sunday afternoon, a servant-girl, who lived with my friend Mrs. C——, came crying to the house, and implored the use of my canoe and paddles, to cross the lake to see her dying father. The request was instantly granted; but there was no man upon the place to ferry her across, and she could not manage the boat herself—in short, had never been in a canoe in her life.

The girl was deeply distressed. She said that she had got word that her father could scarcely live till she could reach Smith-town; that if she went round by the bridge, she must walk five miles, while if she crossed the lake she could be home in half-an-hour.

I did not much like the angry swell upon the water, but the poor creature was in such grief that I told her, if she was not afraid of venturing with me, I would try and put her over.

She expressed her thanks in the warmest terms, accompanied by a shower of blessings; and I took the paddles and went down to the landing. Jenny was very averse to my *tempting Providence*, as she termed it, and wished that I might get back as safe as I went. However, the old woman launched the canoe for me, pushed us from the shore, and away we went. The wind was in my favour, and I found so little trouble in getting across that I began to laugh at my own timidity. I put the girl on shore, and endeavoured to shape my passage home. But this I found was no easy task. The water was rough, and the wind high, and the strong current, which runs through that part of the lake to the Smith rapids, was dead against me. In vain I laboured to cross this current; it resisted all my efforts, and at each repulse I was carried further down towards the rapids, which were full of sunken rocks, and hard for the strong arm of a man to stem—to the weak hand of a woman their safe passage was impossible. I began to feel rather uneasy at the awkward situation in which I found myself placed, and for some time I made desperate efforts to extricate myself, by paddling with all my might. I soon gave this up, and contented myself by steering the canoe in the path it thought fit to pursue. After drifting down with the current for some little space, until I came opposite a small island, I put out all my strength to gain the land. In this I fortunately succeeded, and getting on shore, I contrived to drag the canoe so far round the headland that I got her out of the current. All now was smooth sailing, and I joyfully answered old Jenny's yells from the landing, that I was safe, and would join her in a few minutes.

This fortunate manœuvre stood me in good stead upon another occasion, when crossing the lake, some weeks after this, in company with a young female friend, during a sudden storm.

Two Indian women, heavily laden with their packs of dried venison, called at the house to borrow the canoe, to join their encampment upon the other side. It so happened that I wanted to send to the mill that afternoon, and the boat could not be returned in time without I went over with the Indian women and brought it back. My young friend was delighted at the idea of the frolic, and as she could both steer and paddle, and the day was calm and bright, though excessively warm, we both agreed to accompany the squaws to the other side, and bring back the canoe.

Mrs. Muskrat had fallen in love with a fine fat kitten, whom the children had called "Buttermilk," and she begged so hard for the little puss, that I presented it to her, rather marvelling how she would contrive to carry it so many miles through the woods, and she loaded with such an enormous pack; when, lo! the squaw took down the bundle, and, in the heart of the piles of dried venison, she deposited the cat in a small basket, giving it a thin slice of the meat to console it for its close confinement. Puss received the donation with piteous mews; it was evident that mice and freedom were preferred by her to venison and the honour of riding on a squaw's back.

The squaws paddled us quickly across, and we laughed and chatted as we bounded over the blue waves, until we were landed in a dark cedar swamp, in the heart of which we found the Indian encampment.

A large party were lounging around the fire, superintending the drying of a quantity of venison which was suspended on forked sticks. Besides the flesh of the deer, a number of muskrats were skinned, and extended as if standing bolt upright before the fire, warming their paws. The appearance they cut was most ludicrous. My young friend pointed to the muskrats, as she sank down, laughing, upon one of the skins.

Old Snow-storm, who was present, imagined that she wanted one of them to eat, and very gravely handed her the unsavoury beast, stick and all.

"Does the old man take me for a cannibal?" she said. "I would as soon eat a child."

Among the many odd things cooking at that fire there was something that had the appearance of a bull-frog.

"What can that be?" she said, directing my eyes to the strange monster. "Surely they don't eat bull-frogs!"

This sally was received by a grunt of approbation from Snow-storm; and, though Indians seldom forget their dignity so far as to laugh, he for once laid aside his stoical gravity, and, twirling the thing round with a stick, burst into a hearty peal.

"*Muckakee!* Indian eat *muckakee?*—Ha! ha! Indian no eat *muckakee!* Frenchmans eat his hind legs; they say the speckled beast much good. This no *muckakee!*—the liver of deer, dried—very nice—Indian eat him."

"I wish him much joy of the delicate morsel," said the saucy girl, who was intent upon quizzing and examining every thing in the camp.

We had remained the best part of an hour, when Mrs. Muskrat laid hold of my hand, and leading me through the bush to the shore, pointed up significantly to a cloud, as dark as night, that hung loweringly over the bush.

"Thunder in that cloud—get over the lake—quick, quick, before it breaks." Then motioning for us to jump into the canoe, she threw in the paddles, and pushed us from the shore.

We saw the necessity of haste, and both plied the paddle with diligence to gain the opposite bank, or at least the shelter of the island, before the cloud poured down its fury upon us. We were just in the middle of the current when the first peal of thunder broke with startling nearness over our heads. The storm frowned darkly upon the woods; the rain came down in torrents; and there were we exposed to its utmost fury in the middle of a current too strong for us to stem.

"What shall we do? We shall be drowned!" said my young friend, turning her pale, tearful face towards me.

"Let the canoe float down the current till we get close to the island; then run her into the land. I saved myself once before by this plan."

We did so, and were safe; but there we had to remain, wet to our skins, until the wind and the rain abated sufficiently for us to manage our little craft. "How do you like being upon the lake in a storm like this?" I whispered to my shivering, dripping companion.

"Very well in romance, but terribly dull in reality. We cannot, however, call it a dry joke," continued she, wringing the rain from her dress. "I wish we were suspended over Old Snow-storm's fire with the bull-frog, for I hate a shower-bath with my clothes on."

I took warning by this adventure, never to cross the lake again without a stronger arm than mine in the canoe to steer me safely through the current.

I received much kind attention from my new neighbour, the Rev. W. W——, a truly excellent and pious clergyman of the English Church. The good, white-haired old man expressed the kindest sympathy in all my trials, and strengthened me greatly with his benevolent counsels and gentle charity. Mr. W—— was a true follower of Christ. His Christianity was not confined to his own denomination; and every Sabbath his log cottage was filled with attentive auditors, of all persuasions, who met together to listen to the word of life delivered to them by a Christian minister in the wilderness.

He had been a very fine preacher, and though considerably turned of seventy, his voice was still excellent, and his manner solemn and impressive.

His only son, a young man of twenty-eight years of age,

had received a serious injury in the brain by falling upon a turf-spade from a loft window when a child, and his intellect had remained stationary from that time. Poor Harry was an innocent child; he loved his parents with the simplicity of a child, and all who spoke kindly to him he regarded as friends. Like most persons of his caste of mind, his predilection for pet animals was a prominent instinct. He was always followed by two dogs, whom he regarded with especial favour. The moment he caught your eye, he looked down admiringly upon his four-footed attendants, patting their sleek necks, and murmuring, "Nice dogs—nice dogs." Harry had singled out myself and my little ones as great favourites. He would gather flowers for the girls, and catch butterflies for the boys; while to me he always gave the title of "dear aunt."

It so happened that one fine morning I wanted to walk a couple of miles through the bush, to spend the day with Mrs. C——; but the woods were full of the cattle belonging to the neighbouring settlers, and of these I was terribly afraid. Whilst I was dressing the little girls to accompany me, Harry W—— came in with a message from his mother. "Oh," thought I, "here is Harry W——. He will walk with us through the bush, and defend us from the cattle."

The proposition was made, and Harry was not a little proud of being invited to join our party. We had accomplished half the distance without seeing a single hoof; and I was beginning to congratulate myself upon our unusual luck, when a large red ox, maddened by the stings of the gadflies, came headlong through the brush, tossing up the withered leaves and dried moss with his horns, and making directly towards us. I screamed to my champion for help; but where was he?—running like a frightened chissmunk along the fallen timber, shouting to my eldest girl, at the top of his voice,

"Run, Katty, run!—The bull, the bull! Run, Katty!—

The bull, the bull!"—leaving us poor creatures far behind in the chase.

The bull, who cared not one fig for us, did not even stop to give us a passing stare, and was soon lost among the trees; while our valiant knight never stopped to see what had become of us, but made the best of his way home. So much for taking an innocent for a guard.

The next month most of the militia regiments were disbanded. My husband's services were no longer required at P——, and he once more returned to help to gather in our scanty harvest. Many of the old debts were paid off by his hard-saved pay; and though all hope of continuing in the militia service was at an end, our condition was so much improved that we looked less to the dark than to the sunny side of the landscape.

The potato crop was gathered in, and I had collected my store of dandelion roots for our winter supply of coffee, when one day brought a letter to my husband from the Governor's secretary, offering him the situation of sheriff of the V—— district. Though perfectly unacquainted with the difficulties and responsibilities of such an important office, my husband looked upon it as a gift sent from heaven to remove us from the sorrows and poverty with which we were surrounded in the woods.

Once more he bade us farewell; but it was to go and make ready a home for us, that we should no more be separated from each other.

Heartily did I return thanks to God that night for all his mercies to us; and Sir George Arthur was not forgotten in those prayers.

From B——, my husband wrote to me to make what haste I could in disposing of our crops, household furniture, stock, and farming implements; and to prepare myself and the children to join him on the first fall of snow that would make the roads practicable for sleighing. To facilitate this object, he sent me a box of clothing, to make up for myself and the children.

For seven years I had lived out of the world entirely; my person had been rendered coarse by hard work and exposure to the weather. I looked double the age I really was, and my hair was already thickly sprinkled with gray. I clung to my solitude. I did not like to be dragged from it to mingle in gay scenes, in a busy town, and with gayly-dressed people. I was no longer fit for the world; I had lost all relish for the pursuits and pleasures which are so essential to its votaries; I was contented to live and die in obscurity.

My dear Emilia rejoiced, like a true friend, in my changed prospects, and came up to help me to cut clothes for the children, and to assist me in preparing them for the journey.

I succeeded in selling off our goods and chattels much better than I expected. My old friend, Mr. W——, who was a new comer, became the principal purchaser, and when Christmas arrived I had not one article left upon my hands save the bedding, which it was necessary to take with us.

# CHAPTER XIII.

## THE MAGIC SPELL.

NEVER did eager British children look for the first violets and primroses of spring with more impatience than my baby boys and girls watched, day after day, for the first snow-flakes that were to form the road to convey them to their absent father.

"Winter never means to come this year. It will never snow again!" exclaimed my eldest boy, turning from the window on Christmas-day, with the most rueful aspect that ever greeted the broad, gay beams of the glorious sun. It was like a spring day. The little lake in front of the window glittered like a mirror of silver, set in its dark frame of pine woods.

I, too, was wearying for the snow, and was tempted to think that it did not come as early as usual, in order to disappoint us. But I kept this to myself, and comforted the expecting child with the oft-repeated assertion that it would certainly snow upon the morrow.

But the morrow came and passed away, and many other morrows, and the same mild, open weather prevailed. The last night of the old year was ushered in with furious storms of wind and snow; the rafters of our log cabin shook beneath the violence of the gale, which swept up from the lake like a lion roaring for its prey, driving the snow-flakes through every open crevice, of which there were not a few, and powdering the floor until it rivalled in whiteness the ground without.

"Oh, what a dreadful night!" we cried, as we huddled, shivering, around the old broken stove. "A person abroad in the woods to-night would be frozen. Flesh and blood could not long stand this cutting wind."

"It reminds me of the commencement of a laughable extempore ditty," said I to my young friend, A. C——, who was staying with me, "composed by my husband, during the first very cold night we spent in Canada:

"Oh, the cold of Canada nobody knows,
The fire burns our shoes without warming our toes;
Oh, dear, what shall we do?
Our blankets are thin, and our noses are blue—
Our noses are blue, and our blankets are thin,
It's at zero without, and we 're freezing within!
(*Chorus.*) Oh, dear, what shall we do?

"But, joking apart, my dear A——, we ought to be very thankful that we are not travelling this night to B——."

"But to-morrow," said my eldest boy, lifting up his curly head from my lap. "It will be fine to-morrow, and we shall see dear papa again."

In this hope he lay down on his little bed upon the floor, and was soon fast asleep; perhaps dreaming of that eagerly-anticipated journey, and of meeting his beloved father.

Sleep was a stranger to my eyes. The tempest raged so furiously without that I was fearful the roof would be carried off the house, or that the chimney would take fire. The night was far advanced when old Jenny and myself retired to bed.

My boy's words were prophetic; that was the last night I ever spent in the bush—in the dear forest home which I had loved in spite of all the hardships which we had endured since we pitched our tent in the backwoods. It was the birthplace of my three boys, the school of high resolve and energetic action, in which we had learned to meet calmly, and successfully to battle with, the ills of life. Nor did I leave it without many regretful tears, to mingle once more with a world to whose usages, during my long solitude, I had become almost a stranger, and to whose praise or blame I felt alike indifferent.

When the day dawned, the whole forest scenery lay glittering in a mantle of dazzling white; the sun shone brightly, the heavens were intensely blue, but the cold was so severe that every article of food had to be thawed before we could get our breakfast. The very blankets that covered us during the night were stiff with our frozen breath. "I hope the sleighs won't come to-day," I cried; "we should be frozen on the long journey."

About noon two sleighs turned into our clearing. Old Jenny ran screaming into the room, "The masther has sent for us at last! The sleighs are come! Fine large sleighs, and illigant teams of horses! Och, and it's a cowld day for the wee things to lave the bush."

The snow had been a week in advance of us at B——, and my husband had sent up the teams to remove us. The children jumped about, and laughed aloud for joy. Old Jenny did not know whether to laugh or cry, but she set about helping me to pack up trunks and bedding as fast as our cold hands would permit.

In the midst of the confusion, my brother arrived, like a good genius, to our assistance, declaring his determination to take us down to B—— himself in his large lumber-sleigh. This was indeed joyful news. In less than three hours he despatched the hired sleighs with their loads, and we all stood together in the empty house, striving to warm our hands over the embers of the expiring fire.

How cold and desolate every object appeared! The small windows, half blocked up with snow, scarcely allowed a glimpse of the declining sun to cheer us with his serene aspect. In spite of the cold, several kind friends had waded through the deep snow to say, "God bless you!—Good-bye;" while a group of silent Indians stood together, gazing upon our proceedings with an earnestness which showed that they were not uninterested in the scene. As we passed out to the sleigh, they pressed forward, and silently held out their hands, while the squaws kissed me and the little ones with tearful eyes. They had been true friends to us in our dire necessity, and I returned their mute farewell from my very heart.

Mr. S—— sprang into the sleigh. One of our party was missing. "Jenny!" shouted my brother, at the top of his voice, "it is too cold to keep your mistress and the little children waiting."

"Och, shure thin, it is I that am comin'!" returned the old body, as she issued from the house.

Shouts of laughter greeted her appearance. The figure she cut upon that memorable day I shall never forget. My brother dropped the reins upon the horses' necks, and fairly roared. Jenny was about to commence her journey to the front in three hats. Was it to protect her from the cold? Oh, no; Jenny was not afraid of the cold! She could have eaten her breakfast on the north side of an iceberg, and always dispensed with shoes, during the most severe of our Canadian winters. It was to protect these precious articles from injury.

Our good neighbour, Mrs. W——, had presented her with an old sky-blue drawn-silk bonnet, as a parting benediction. This, by way of distinction, for she never had possessed such an article of luxury as a silk bonnet in her life, Jenny had placed over the coarse calico cap, with its full furbelow of the same yellow, ill-washed, homely material, next to her head, over this, as second in degree, a sun-burnt straw hat, with faded pink ribbons, just showed its broken rim and tawdry trimmings; and, to crown all, and serve as a guard to the rest, a really serviceable gray beaver bonnet, once mine, towered up as high as the celebrated crown in which brother Peter figures in Swift's "Tale of a Tub."

"Mercy, Jenny! Why, old woman, you don't mean to go with us that figure?"

"Och, my dear heart! I've no bandbox to kape the cowld from desthroying my illigant bonnets," returned Jenny, laying her hand upon the side of the sleigh.

"Go back, Jenny; go back," cried my brother. "For God's sake take all that tomfoolery from off your head. We shall be the laughing-stock of every village we pass through."

"Och, shure now, Mr. S——, who'd think of looking at an owld crathur like me! It's only yersel' that would notice the like."

"All the world, every body would look at you, Jenny. I believe that you put on those hats to draw the attention of all the young fellows that we shall happen to meet on the road. Ha, Jenny!"

With an air of offended dignity, the old woman returned to the house to re-arrange her toilet, and provide for the safety of her "illigant bonnets," one of which she suspended to the strings of her cloak, while she carried the third dangling in her hand; and no persuasion of mine would induce her to put them out of sight.

Many painful and conflicting emotions agitated my mind, but found no utterance in words, as we entered the forest path, and I looked my last upon that humble home consecrated by the memory of a thousand sorrows. Every object had become endeared to me during my long exile from civilized life. I loved the lonely lake, with its magnificent belt of dark pines sighing in the breeze; the cedar swamp, the summer home of my dark Indian friends; my own dear little garden, with its rugged snake-fence, which I had helped Jenny to place with my own hands, and which I had assisted the faithful woman in cultivating for the last three years, where I had so often braved the tormenting mosquitoes, black-flies, and intense heat, to provide vegetables for the use of the family. Even the cows, that had given a breakfast for the last time to my children, were now regarded with mournful affection. A poor labourer stood in the doorway of the deserted house, holding my noble water-dog, Rover, in a string. The poor fellow gave a joyous bark as my eyes fell upon him.

"James J——, take care of my dog."

"Never fear, ma'am, he shall bide with me as long as he lives."

"He and the Indians at least feel grieved for our departure," I thought. Love is so scarce in this world that we ought to prize it, however lowly the source from whence it flows.

We accomplished only twelve miles of our journey that night. The road lay through the bush, and along the banks of the grand, rushing, foaming Otonabee river, the wildest and most beautiful of forest streams. We slept at the house of kind friends, and early in the morning resumed our long journey, but minus one of our party. Our old favourite cat, Peppermint, had made her escape from the basket in which she had been confined, and had scampered off, to the great grief of the children.

As we passed Mrs. H——'s house, we called for dear Addie. Mr. H—— brought her in his arms to the gate, well wrapped up in a large fur cape and a warm woollen shawl.

"You are robbing me of my dear little girl," he said. "Mrs. H—— is absent; she told me not to part with her if you should call; but I could not detain her without your consent. Now that you have seen her, allow me to keep her for a few months longer!"

Addie was in the sleigh. I put my arm around her. felt I had my child again, and I secretly rejoiced in the possession of my own. I sincerely thanked him for his kindness, and Mr. S—— drove on.

At Mr. R——'s, we found a parcel from dear Emilia, containing a plum-cake and other good things for the children. Her kindness never flagged.

We crossed the bridge over the Otonabee, in the rising town of Peterborough, at eight o'clock in the morning. Winter had now set in fairly. The children were glad to huddle together in the bottom of the sleigh, under the buffalo skins and blankets; all but my eldest boy, who, just turned of five years old, was enchanted with all he heard and saw, and continued to stand up and gaze around him. Born in the forest, which he had never quitted before, the sight of a town was such a novelty that he could find no words wherewith to express his astonishment.

"Are the houses come to see one another?" he asked. "How did they all meet here?"

The question greatly amused his uncle, who took some pains to explain to him the difference between town and country. During the day, we got rid of old Jenny and her bonnets, whom we found a very refractory travelling companion; as wilful, and far more difficult to manage than a young child. Fortunately, we overtook the sleighs with the furniture, and Mr. S—— transferred Jenny to the care of one of the drivers; an arrangement that proved satisfactory to all parties.

We had been most fortunate in obtaining comfortable lodgings for the night. The evening had closed in so intensely cold, that although we were only two miles from C——, Addie was so much affected by it that the child lay sick and pale in my arms, and, when spoken to, seemed scarcely conscious of our presence.

My brother jumped from the front seat, and came round to look at her. "That child is ill with the cold; we must stop somewhere to warm her, or she will hardly hold out till we get to the inn at C——."

We were just entering the little village of A——, in the vicinity of the court-house, and we stopped at a pretty green cottage, and asked permission to warm the children. A stout, middle-aged woman came to the sleigh, and in the kindest manner requested us to alight.

"I think I know that voice," I said. "Surely it cannot be Mrs. S——, who once kept the —— hotel at C——?"

"Mrs. Moodie, you are welcome," said the excellent woman, bestowing upon me a most friendly embrace; "you and your children. I am heartily glad to see you again after so many years. God bless you all!"

Nothing could exceed the kindness and hospitality of this generous woman; she would not hear of our leaving her that night, and, directing my brother to put up his horses in her stable, she made up an excellent fire in a large bedroom, and helped me to undress the little ones who were already asleep, and to warm and feed the rest before we put them to bed.

This meeting gave me real pleasure. In their station of life, I seldom have found a more worthy couple than this American and his wife; and, having witnessed so many of their acts of kindness, both to ourselves and others, I entertained for them a sincere respect and affection, and truly rejoiced that Providence had once more led me to the shelter of their roof.

Mr. S—— was absent, but I found little Mary—the sweet

child who used to listen with such delight to Moodie's flute—grown up into a beautiful girl; and the baby that was, a fine child of eight years old. The next morning was so intensely cold that my brother would not resume the journey until past ten o'clock, and even then it was a hazardous experiment.

We had not proceeded four miles before the horses were covered with icicles. Our hair was frozen as white as Old Time's solitary forelock, our eyelids stiff, and every limb aching with cold.

"This will never do," said my brother, turning to me; "the children will freeze. I never felt the cold more severe than this."

"Where can we stop?" said I; "we are miles from C——, and I see no prospect of the weather becoming milder."

"Yes, yes; I know, by the very intensity of the cold, that a change is at hand. We seldom have more than three very severe days running, and this is the third. At all events, it is much warmer at night in this country than during the day; the wind drops, and the frost is more bearable. I know a worthy farmer who lives about a mile ahead; he will give us house-room for a few hours, and we will resume our journey in the evening. The moon is at full; and it will be easier to wrap the children up, and keep them warm when they are asleep. Shall we stop at Old Woodruff's?"

"With all my heart." My teeth were chattering with the cold, and the children were crying over their aching fingers at the bottom of the sleigh.

A few minutes' ride brought us to a large farm-house, surrounded by commodious sheds and barns. A fine orchard opposite, and a yard well stocked with fat cattle and sheep, sleek geese, and plethoric-looking swine, gave promise of a land of abundance and comfort. My brother ran into the house to see if the owner was at home, and presently returned, accompanied by the staunch Canadian yeoman and his daughter, who gave us a truly hearty welcome, and assisted in removing the children from the sleigh to the cheerful fire, that made all bright and cozy within.

Our host was a shrewd, humorous-looking Yorkshireman. His red, weather beaten face, and tall, athletic figure, bent as it was with hard labour, gave indications of great personal strength; and a certain knowing twinkle in his small, clear gray eyes, which had been acquired by long dealing with the world, with a quiet, sarcastic smile that lurked round the corners of his large mouth, gave you the idea of a man who could not easily be deceived by his fellows; one who, though no rogue himself, was quick in detecting the roguery of others. His manners were frank and easy, and he was such a hospitable entertainer that you felt at home with him in a minute.

"Well, how are you, Mr. S——?" cried the farmer, shaking my brother heartily by the hand. "Toiling in the bush still, eh?"

"Just in the same place."

"And the wife and children?"

"Hearty. Some half-dozen have been added to the flock since you were our way."

"So much the better—so much the better. The more the merrier, Mr. S——; children are riches in this country."

"I know not how that may be; I find it hard to clothe and feed mine."

"Wait till they grow up; they will be brave helps to you then. The price of labour—the price of labour, Mr. S——, is the destruction of the farmer."

"It does not seem to trouble you much, Woodruff," said my brother, glancing round the well-furnished apartment.

"My son and S—— do it all," cried the old man. "Of course the girls help in busy times, and take care of the dairy, and we hire occasionally; but small as the sum is which is expended in wages during seed-time and harvest, I feel it, I can tell you."

"You are married again, Woodruff?"

"No, sir," said the farmer, with a peculiar smile; "not yet:" which seemed to imply the probability of such an event. "That tall gal is my eldest daughter; she manages the house, and an excellent housekeeper she is. But I cannot keep her for ever." With a knowing wink, "Gals will think of getting married, and seldom consult the wishes of their parents upon the subject when once they have taken the notion into their heads. But 'tis natural, Mr. S——, it is natural; we did just the same when we were young."

My brother looked laughingly towards the fine, handsome young woman, as she placed upon the table hot water, whiskey, and a huge plate of plum-cake, which did not lack a companion, stored with the finest apples which the orchard could produce

The young girl looked down, and blushed.

"Oh, I see how it is, Woodruff! You will soon lose your daughter. I wonder that you have kept her so long. But who are these young ladies?" he continued, as three girls very demurely entered the room.

"The two youngest are my darters, by my last wife, who, I fear, mean soon to follow the bad example of their sister. The other *lady*," said the old man, with a reverential air, "is a *particular* friend of my eldest darter's."

My brother laughed slyly, and the old man's cheek took a deeper glow as he stooped forward to mix the punch.

"You said that these two young ladies, Woodruff, were by your last wife. Pray how many wives have you had?"

"Only three. It is impossible, they say in my country, to have too much of a good thing."

"So I suppose you think," said my brother, glancing first at the old man and then towards Miss Smith. "Three wives! You have been a fortunate man, Woodruff, to survive them all."

"Ah, have I not, Mr. S——? but to tell you the truth, I have been both lucky and unlucky in the wife way," and then he told us the history of his several ventures in matrimony, with which I shall not trouble my readers.

When he had concluded, the weather was somewhat milder, the sleigh was ordered to the door, and we proceeded on our journey, resting for the night at a small village about twenty miles from B——, rejoicing that the long distance which separated us from the husband and father was diminished to a few miles, and that, with the blessing of Providence, we should meet on the morrow.

About noon we reached the distant town, and were met at the inn by him whom one and all so ardently longed to see. He conducted us to a pretty, neat cottage, which he had prepared for our reception, and where we found old Jenny already arrived. With great pride the old woman conducted me over the premises, and showed me the furniture "the masther" had bought; especially recommending to my notice a china tea-service, which she considered the most wonderful acquisition of the whole.

"Och! who would have thought, a year ago, misthress dear, that we should be living in a mansion like this, and ating off raal chaney? It is but yestherday that we were hoeing praties in the field."

"Yes, Jenny, God has been very good to us, and I hope that we shall never learn to regard with indifference the many benefits which we have received at His hands."

Reader! it is not my intention to trouble you with the sequel of our history. I have given you a faithful picture of a life in the backwoods of Canada, and I leave you to draw from it your own conclusions. To the poor, industrious workingman it presents many advantages; to the poor gentleman, *none!* The former works hard, puts up with coarse, scanty fare, and submits, with a good grace, to hardships that would kill a domesticated animal at home. Thus he becomes independent, inasmuch as the land that he has cleared finds him in the common necessaries of life; but it seldom, if ever, in remote situations, accomplishes more than this. The gentleman can neither work so hard, live so coarsely, nor endure so many privations as his poorer but more fortunate neighbour. Unaccustomed to manual labour, his services in the field are not of a nature to secure for him a profitable return. The task is new to him, he knows not how to perform it well; and, conscious of his deficiency, he expends his little means in hiring labour, which his bush-farm can never repay. Difficulties increase, debts grow upon him, he struggles in vain to extricate himself, and finally sees his family sink into hopeless ruin.

If these sketches should prove the means of deterring one family from sinking their property, and shipwrecking all their hopes, by going to reside in the backwoods of Canada, I shall consider myself amply repaid for revealing the secrets of the prison-house, and feel that I have not toiled and suffered in the wilderness in vain.

## THE MAPLE-TREE.

### A CANADIAN SONG.

HAIL to the pride of the forest—hail
To the maple, tall and green;
It yields a treasure which ne'er shall fail
While leaves on its boughs are seen.
When the moon shines bright,
On the wintry night,
And silvers the frozen snow;
And echo dwells
On the jingling bells
As the sleighs dart to and fro;
Then it brightens the mirth
Of the social hearth
With its red and cheery glow.

Afar, 'mid the bosky forest shades,
It lifts its tall head on high;
When the crimson-tinted evening fades
From the glowing saffron sky;
When the sun's last beams
Light up woods and streams,
And brighten the gloom below;
And the deer springs by
With his flashing eye,
And the shy, swift-footed doe;
And the sad winds chide
In the branches wide,
With a tender plaint of woe.

The Indian leans on its rugged trunk,
With the bow in his red right-hand,
And mourns that his race, like a stream, has sunk
From the glorious forest land.

But, blithe and free,
The maple-tree,
Still tosses to sun and air
Its thousand arms,
While in countless swarms
The wild bee revels there;
But soon not a trace
Of the red man's race
Shall be found in the landscape fair.

When the snows of winter are melting fast,
And the sap begins to rise,
And the biting breath of the frozen blast
Yields to the spring's soft sighs,
Then away to the wood,
For the maple, good,
Shall unlock its honied store;
And boys and girls,
With their sunny curls,
Bring their vessels brimming o'er
With the luscious flood
Of the brave tree's blood,
Into caldrons deep to pour.

The blaze from the sugar-bush gleams red;
Far down in the forest dark,
A ruddy glow on the trees is shed,
That lights up their rugged bark;
And with merry shout,
The busy rout
Watch the sap as it bubbles high;
And they talk of the cheer
Of the coming year,
And the jest and the song pass by;
And brave tales of old
Round the fire are told,
That kindle youth's beaming eye.

Hurra! for the sturdy maple-tree!
Long may its green branch wave;
In native strength sublime and free,
Meet emblem for the brave.

May the nation's peace
With its growth increase,
And its worth be widely spread;
For it lifts not in vain
To the sun and rain
Its tall, majestic head.
May it grace our soil,
And reward our toil,
Till the nation's heart is dead!

Reader! my task is ended.

THE END.

Stereotyped by Billin & Brothers, No. 20 North William-street.

www.ingramcontent.com/pod-product-compliance
Lightning Source LLC
LaVergne TN
LVHW050530100826
845148LV00002B/509

*9781425519254*